MW00443314

Soul *to* Sole

Soul to Sole Co-Parenting with a
Difference in the "NEW FAMILY"

....

*Helpful Ways of Getting Through the Divorce
and to a Happier Co Parenting*

Dorothy O'Neill Psy.D

© Dorothy O'Neill Psy.D 2021

ISBN: 978-1-09838-832-4

eBook ISBN: 978-1-09838-833-1

All rights reserved. This book or any portion thereof may not be reproduced or used in any manner whatsoever without the express written permission of the publisher except for the use of brief quotations in a book review.

This book is dedicated to my children Emily and Sophia, who grew up in a world of divorce and came out as amazing young women, and their father, Ron, who was willing to work as a team

. . . .

ACKNOWLEDGMENTS

I would not have written this book without the many people who acknowledged how I co-parented with my children's father in the early years, and throughout their school experience.

It was through many of you that I realized that this was not the norm and you encouraged me to write about how to co-parent after a divorce and here it is!

I started writing on this topic in my Psy.D program with Dr. Rajeswari Natrajan-Tyagi who also encouraged me to continue.

Well, here I am years later and finally coming to the end of the book. I had help along the way and want to thank the friends and helpers that joined me. First, I have to add my sister Patsy as she has made me commit to putting her in every book.

Allen Anca, a young man who wants to enter the field of psychology, for finding research articles. Stephanie Root for doing the first proofreading and encouraging me to continue. Charlotte Jackson for working beside me in the final draft to get the book ready for print, Bart Carey for his insight into a better divorce. Izabella Zitney who jumped in at the end to pull the pieces together. And last but not least, Tim Brown for his thoughtful final review and insight from the perspective of a reader.

It has been a labor of love and I hope this book will encourage divorced couples to share their children with kindness and grace.

FOREWORD: MRS. STEPHANIE ROOT

Like ice cream, families come in a variety of flavors!

However, unlike ice cream, the one thing that remains true for families is the need to constantly work together and communicate to ensure a healthy environment for all. Being introduced to Dorothy approximately 20 years ago in a school setting, I was blessed with the opportunity to see how important co-parenting was and how it impacted the family structure and the success of the children.

I had the pleasure of working with both of Dorothy's girls throughout their elementary and high school years as an educational coach. Her knowledge, love for her family, and dedication to work hard was always apparent. Dorothy was always open and willing to work as a collaborative team, including her spouse, to help her family succeed. Although there was a divorce, they worked well together in order to raise their daughters.

Dorothy has a passion for life and the drive to do what is right. She has always valued family as her most important asset, especially the children. Raising them in a happy, healthy environment with both parents equally present and cooperative was key. Witnessing this unique, highly recommended union of co-parenting, I was able to grow and learn the importance of putting differences and hurt aside in order to parent in a manner that contributes to a family unit and young adults who can thrive in the world.

As you read the book, keep in mind that the children are always first despite the differences of the parents. The differences are addressed and the fact that this is not an easy process for the adults to experience is recognized. There are practical solutions and ideas for parents who are striving to co-parent and doing what is best for the children.

As an educator for 25 years, I have seen families struggle and children who pay the price for the adult's behavior.

Consider co-parenting with an open mind and allow the words of the author to speak to your heart. Enjoy!

Stephanie Root, M.Ed.

Contents

WHY YOU NEED THIS BOOK

This book is for divorcing couples that want to be the best parents they can be. Some couples will need to work on themselves before they can co-parent successfully, and that's okay- but the goal should be that children do not have to suffer because of the decision's that we adults make. It is regrettable that we must have this conversation, but divorce has become so much more common as of late and the speed in which couples are reconnecting with another partner is staggering. This leads to complicated and difficult relationships that directly impact the children.

Mutual respect must be developed and enacted as soon as possible.

Many children in the US live with one parent and must navigate not only the change in living arrangements but also adjust to the change in the parents' behavior. These children often suffer due to the lack of consistency and role-modeling of healthy relationships. This leads them into their own difficulties as adults.

The purpose of writing this book is not to write another book on the rules of working in divorce or what the standard operating procedure is today, but to help find another way that WORKS for the sake of the children involved.

My life was not what I had expected. I envisioned the "happy" family with a husband and two kids, a beautiful home, successful careers, and many happy years ahead of us, all wrapped up in what others call "The American Dream." However, this was not the case. After a bitter few months divorcing and many hardships, I was able to start looking at what I could do to keep my children from the harsh situations that often occur because of divorce and nurture them in a way that demonstrated how to have a healthy relationship with both parents, despite their differences.

I want to be able to help couples see that although we are meant to legally divorce, finalize days that we can see our children, and split holidays and birthdays, **the children should not become a commodity of our union.**

But they do; they become pawns and players in a game that they did not choose to enter.

Parents have an obligation to protect their children and to make sure they grow up to be strong and well-adjusted adults.

Even in the worst situation (barring abuse of any kind), this should be able to be accomplished.

WE MUST LOVE OUR CHILDREN MORE THAN WE HATE OUR PARTNER

This is the first stage of healing, for us, our children, and the future of the family. You don't have to learn everything at once but must start somewhere.

CHAPTER 1

This is a Beginning, and an End

· ·

Being the recipient of a divorce is not easy, egos get burned, hearts get broken, and lives get turned upside down. It is a difficult time, not knowing what comes next, and how to adjust to a new normal, how to fit into a different life, one that is foreign and unknown.

However, this is the same for our children; they are discovering a 'new normal' in a different life, one that is also foreign and unknown. It is this fact that must make us take a moment to consider how we can navigate this while doing the best we can for our children. There is a role that we must play; as a parent we have to do the best we can to make sure that no child is caught in what can be a tsunami of hate and hurt.

Children pick up on the emotions we give off, both the positive and the negative, therefore we cannot set a seed of anger and hurt towards our spouse that continues throughout the child's life.

Parents should not want to be a party to the negative situation

Children are growing, developing, and maturing; they have enough to deal with as they experience childhood, adolescence, and young adulthood. This will vary depending on their age group, but from toddlers learning how to crawl, interact, and cope with emotions, to teenagers dealing with a change in hormones, change in body image, and change in social habits - our children have enough on their plate. Let them have these experiences without pushing our own issues onto them. We owe them that much; as their parents we should feel that if we want healthy adults, we must be the first defense in helping our children grow up safe and healthy, whether our family is nuclear or separated.

In this book you will be able to read about working as a team in a variety of ways that surpass the ideas of the standard legal system, or the old-school way of co-parenting that has been utilized and adopted for a lifetime.

PARENTING HAS TO CHANGE IN THIS NEW ERA OF DIVORCE

When parents act out of anger, tension increases in children of all ages and they are affected. Parents lose sight of reason, balance, and understanding as they enter the arena of the divorcing world. Sadly, too many marriages are ending in divorce, and therefore a new plan needs to be implemented on how co-parenting works and how the family unit deals with the pain that results at the end of a dream.

Parents lose sight of reason, balance, and understanding as they enter the arena of the divorcing world

Abusive and violent relationships are the exception and need to be addressed differently. This program is not for abusive and violent relationships and the teachings of this book cannot be applied to those relationships. Individuals must take care of their safety and the safety of their children first and at all costs.

CHAPTER 2

The End of an Era

. . . .

O nce upon a time, you chose this person to experience life with, they cannot be all bad. That's not to say it writes off any wrongdoing they (or you) may have done, or it ignores the fact that your relationship with them has significantly changed over the years, but there is a history you both share and life is too short to only focus on the worst in people. If you look for the good and take this phase in your life with positive intent, then outside of the realm of abuse, there is no situation that cannot be worked through.

It is not about being a happy couple; it is about being happy parents. You and your partner may be very different, but those differences don't stop you from loving your children with all your hearts and working towards a happy family environment by co-parenting in harmony.

. . . .

It is not about being a happy couple; it is about being happy parents.

. . . .

Today [in North America] we average one divorce every 13 seconds, this equates to 277 divorces per hour, 6,646 per day, 46,523 per week, and 2,419,196 per year.[17] Given this, it has become vital that couples learn and understand a new set of relationship behaviors that apply post-marriage. These behaviors need to include the ability to put the needs of the children first, work as a team for the benefit of the children, function in ways that unite the needs of the "new family," act in a way that promotes a cooperative relationship, that excludes romance, intimacy, and common abode, but does not follow the social norm of having to remove all the relationships after a divorce. We no longer live in a society where divorce is the exception and not the norm.

With divorces come many lifestyle changes and problems. Children become more vulnerable and the probability of getting into trouble grows. The disruption divorce causes in the household often leaves the children open to getting into trouble at school, experiencing stress-related illness, and to perpetuate divorce for themselves as adults. The ability for couples to co-parent after the divorce becomes a difficult process.[27]

The greatest gift a couple can give their children is to be kind to each other after the divorce. In a good divorce the family remains intact. The parents continue to be reasonable for the emotional, economical, and physical needs of the children.[1] The couple learns to navigate into a cooperative relationship that permits the bonds of kinship with, and through, the children. Both spouses can achieve collective strategies that work for both in a harmonious setting.

The greatest gift a couple can give their children is to be kind to each other after the divorce.

This is a new type of relationship though; divorce has only recently become both normalized and accepted. That's not to say separations weren't happening before this, but there was a different social impact than there is now, but it means there are limited studies regarding this type of relationship. Hence, it is hard to know what it looks like without a bit of guidance.

This guidance often comes in the form of books, many of which provide rules that tell you how to behave, what not to say, and how to work together. What these books do not take into consideration though is that there must still be a connection to what the family structure once was.

Although this is not common yet, I have met many couples that have been able to do it, and it has made for a better environment for everyone involved, including both the "grown-ups" and the children. It is not about acting as though the past did not exist but acknowledging that there was a family structure before, and there will be a family structure again. It is your job to decide what you want that new structure to look like, and what you are prepared to do in order to help the family get there.

I will repeat myself when I say, the greatest gift a couple can give their children is to be kind to each other after the divorce. Toys, money, trips to Disneyland, clothes, and stuff does not come close to a child seeing their parents work together to make the situation the best it can be.

CHAPTER 3

The Attachment

· ·

T he attachment we bring into the relationship with our children comes first from the one we have with our own parents. This is important to be aware of because it means the relationship you create with your children is going to impact all their future relationships. "Adults that were secure in their romantic relationships recalled childhood relationships with their parents as being safe.[15] These adults recalled a household of affection and caring with an acceptance of who they were." Healthy parent relationships can be the making of well-developed social, cognitive, and emotional skills[19] as well as overall more balanced adults. Knowing this, it is integral—not just for the sake of our children's current state, but also their future state—that we encourage continued healthy relationships with both parents during the divorce.

The attachment you bring into the relationship comes from the one you have with your parents

The relationships we have with our children shape what is called their attachment style. Typically, people fit within three types of attachments: secure attachment, anxious-resistant attachment, and avoidant attachment.[19]

These attachment styles evolved from John Bowlby's evolutionary theory of attachment. Bowlby (1907-1990) was a British psychoanalyst who believed mental health and problems with behavior could be attributed to early childhood. [19]

A securely attached child still shows distress upon being separated from their primary caregiver but can be easily comforted. [19] An example of this would be a child being dropped off at preschool. The child might grip the parent and look distressed or be concerned when walking into the classroom but after a few moments, the child settles down and starts to play. At the end of the day, when the parent returns to the child, the child greets the parent with content. This child is happy to see the parent return but without feeling anxiety.

Parents that grow up as a securely attached child know how to self-soothe, and although they will still have to work through a divorce, they at least enter that new world with typically less trauma or stress. In difficult situations, this parent will have the ability to process their own feelings with a better understanding rather than go straight to the victim mode. The victim mode is when you feel responsible for everything and feel you are doing everything alone.

An anxious-resistant attachment child has a greater level of distress when separated from the caregiver. [19] Taking this type of child to preschool can be stressful; at drop-off the child grips the parent's leg, crying and distressed. As the child enters the classroom, unable to settle down, looking back, he/she remains distressed for most of the time. When the parent returns to pick up the child, they display their anger, they show signs of aggressive behavior by kicking, punching, and other forms of physical harm. This behavior reflects the frustration that the child is feeling because they were left at school, the child feels the need to "punish the parent".

The avoidant attachment child shows no stress or minimal stress when separated from the parent. [19] This same child at the pre-school would run in with no goodbyes, no tears, and no distress. This child at the end of the day stays and plays with the other children, does not run up to the returning parent, and treats the parent as if they were not there, actively avoiding the parent. Many parents see this as a secure child; however, a secure child has a measure of healthy anxiety and an ability to self-soothe while working through the change of attending school for the first time.

Growing up as an anxious, resistant child leaves a parent with an inability to attach when needed and address the needs of the child first. In a divorce, the child needs a parent that can regulate their own emotions. In parents that have this attachment style, they will feel intense emotions such as rejection and abandonment with the divorce, which in turn leads to anger. A feeling of insecurity leads to jealousy and does not allow the parent to keep the focus on the child.

Building on Bowlby's work on attachment, a fourth attachment was added.

The disorganized-disoriented attachment is the most extreme of the insecure attachment styles. This attachment reflects a child who does not follow any predictable pattern of attachment behavior.[20] This child would have grown up in a frightening household—often being mistreated by the caregiver, there could be miscommunication of feelings, and often unattainable goals of the child. The child understands he or she is not safe and believes the parent is to be feared.

One of the most important gifts we should give our children is to help them develop healthy attachments. How we do this is to be consistent with what they experience, showing the child that they are not abandoned, and the love that both parents had for them before the divorce is the same love that they have after the divorce.

One of the most important gifts we should give our children is to help them develop healthy attachments.

Understanding the development of your child before the divorce can help you understand how they might fare in the changes taking place. Erik Erikson's[18] stages of development provide you with an opportunity to look back, or to see presently where your child is in their development. In addition, it also allows one to see what is needed to grow up safe and secure in these difficult times of divorce.

Although these stages are important, no child can develop 100 percent trust or 100 percent doubt; there needs to be a balance between the two opposing sides.[25] Do not expect that your child will fit perfectly into one box. They will be somewhere on a hypothetical scale. The below provides a rough, but helpful, outline of these development stages.

Stage 1: Trust vs. Mistrust

Infancy (birth to 18 months)

Conflict for the child: Trust vs. Mistrust

Significant Event: Feeding and nurturing

At this stage of your child's life, they are completely dependent on you. Developing trust is based on the kind of caregiving they receive. At this age they receive whatever they need—nurturing, food, love and affection, and safety- directly from the parent or caregiver. This beginning stage in the life of a child is when they learn to trust the adults in their lives. The caregiver is consistent and emotionally reliable. This is a time in the child's life when they are completely dependent on their parents. At this stage if the parent fails to deliver these needs, the child will learn that the world is not safe – but if this stage is fulfilled, it will create the necessary foundation of trust for the child to have for their parent.[18]

An example of a child not having these needs met would be a child that is left in their crib for long periods with no attention, or at times cry for attention for needs not given.

Trust is such a major player in a relationship and, when not developed in early life, it can create fear. Without Mom and Dad together, there is a missing piece, and kids do not have the knowledge to fully understand the situation. However, it is possible to help your children successfully develop during this stage if you work together with the co-parent and put the needs of your child first. It is vital they feel loved and prioritized.[18]

Stage 2: Autonomy vs. Shame and Doubt

Early Childhood (2 to 3 years)

Basic Conflict: Autonomy vs. Shame and Doubt

Significant Event: Toilet Training

At this point in the child's life there is a need to develop a sense of personal control and the beginnings of independence. Toilet training is a perfect example of this independence. A child in this age group is trying to develop physical skills, such as small tasks like picking clothes, choosing toys, and food. These tasks need to be age-appropriate, providing some boundaries, as allowing a child to have completely free reign only creates confusion. These boundaries are in place so that the child understands that there are rules.

During this stage, children who have accidents and are made to feel shame will develop self-doubt and will carry this into adulthood. An example of this would be if a child spills a glass of milk and the parent shouts at the child, admonishing them. Having this reaction towards the child, shaming them for the accident, teaches the child that they are inadequate.

In divorce, shame and doubt are often present. If a parent projects this shame onto a child, it can cause them to take on guilt and think that they are party to the problem of the breakup. Given this, it is important that you support your children during this stage, help them to see their value by teaching them independence, and not berate them when they make mistakes. Children that have learned to be autonomous can often see what is going on and process from a developed sense of self in adulthood.[18]

Stage 3: Initiative vs. Guilt

Preschool (3 to 5 years)

Significant Events: Exploration

Basic Conflict: Initiative vs. Guilt

At this stage, children want to affirm that they have some power over their own lives. They do this by directing their play and how they engage in social interactions. There needs to be a balance here. If the child exerts too much power that is met with disfavor, another period of guilt and shame forms – for example, a child that screams for something and keeps going until they get what they want is not learning to have a voice but is learning how to control a parent using guilt. However, with the right balance, children learn a sense of purpose.

Parents often confuse giving too much power to the child is allowing the child to have a voice, but this is often the reason the child becomes out of control.

Guilt is a prevalent emotion between parent and child during divorce and it is important to be aware of how it is being used. Are your children showing that they love one parent more than another? Does Mom or Dad know what they want to share and if they say anything, are they hurting their parents? However, when a child has developed a sense of initiative and can sort out what is okay and what is their role, they can fair the rough waters of the divorce.[18]

Stage 4: Industry vs. Inferiority
School Age (6 to 11 years)

Significant Event: School

Basic Conflict: Industry vs. Inferiority

This is the time in a child's life where they develop the ability to see worth and pride in what they do. The accomplishments build, and the abilities of the child grow. School is a major benchmark of pride in accomplishments. Success in school helps the child build a sense of worth in themselves.

When the child is given affirmations from teachers and parents, they can build competence and belief in their skills. Children that do not receive encouragement from either school or parents will often doubt their own skills.

Inferiority is a sad place for a child to be. It is difficult enough dealing with the situation before divorce occurs. There is so much going on that it is not always possible to affirm the child about all of their accomplishments. Life has changed and each solo parent has a lot on their plate. A child that has developed a sense of industry will seek pride from their own self-worth and feel proud of the work they keep doing despite the difficult time of divorce. [25]

Stage 5: Identity vs. Confusion

Adolescence (12 to 18 year)

Significant Events: Social Relationships

Basic Conflict: Identity vs. Role Confusion

This age is a tough time for teenagers and often turbulent, even without divorcing parents. They need to develop who they are and how they fit into society—with peers, their parents, and family. If they have progressed well through all the other stages, they will be prepared for this phase of their life. When the child has a personal identity of self that is not confused or weak, they can stay true to themselves. During this time the child needs encouragement and reinforcement to develop a congruent personal identity of self. This means they will have a trust and belief in themselves and can identify who they are with a sense of self-worth and understanding. The child will feel secure and able to work through the ups and downs in their life. Children that remain insecure at this stage will be confused about themselves in the future.

Identity is so important as a teenager; these are difficult times to navigate even in a two-parent family. Often at this age, they are leaning towards their peers and what their peers think. In today's society, they are not alone, as many of their friends will be in the same situation at home. If by this age they have developed a sense of identity they will fare better and get through the difficulties and be able to look ahead.

Our personal identity helps guide us in our actions, behaviors, and is the very vessel that guides our beliefs. Although Erikson's theory[18] is well researched and investigated, the exact mechanism for resolving conflict and moving from one stage to the next is not well known. However, it does allow for a broad framework for the development of our life span. The theory also allows us to understand the social nature of human beings and the important influence that social relationships have on development.

Hence, when children are entering the divorcing arena, they need to be equipped with what it takes to get to the finish line. Each of these stages, no matter what age the child is at the onset of the divorce, will help develop a better and healthy child.[18]

> *Our personal identity helps guide us in our actions, behaviors, and is the very vessel that guides our beliefs.*

CHAPTER 4

Divorce and the Legal System

· ·

The longer the conflicting legal process takes, the worse the parents' behavior to each other becomes, and the harder it is for a cooperative co-parenting to be established.[7] It is so important for parents to start as soon as possible to make the transition from couple hood to singlehood, and work on a team approach.

Control is often a major player in the early stage of the divorce process. The partner that was not the initiator of the divorce often feels victimized and feels the need to engage in a power struggle. This puts the initiator in a position of power. Fathers often have a harder time. If the father's not the initiator of the divorce, they have a more difficult time regaining power. I often talk to fathers who feel they have lost control in the court system and often feel they have become marginalized. Father's don't always get a 50/50 split on custody as they would desire, and at times can lose control and involvement with the child's development.

· ·

Control is often a major player in the early stage of the divorce process.

The course of the divorce creates not only a power play but also a heightened anger. Anxiety, diminished communication, sadness, conflict, and depression can affect both parties. The negative impact on the children during this high conflict period has been well established in empirical and clinical literature.[13] A similar study[22] states although the couple experiences the same divorce processing, their perceptual realities may be quite different. The authors also believe two distinct marriages are at play in every marital union. This essentially means that when a couple marries, they bring with them their own individual histories in how they perceive marriage; Hence, it is not surprising for these unique personal qualities and experiences to be the guiding force behind each partner's interpretation of the divorce. The events and circumstances are viewed in two different ways.

Considerable research evidence now suggests it is not the divorce that is the most damaging for the children, but the process by which parents continue to interact after the divorce.

In high conflict families not only does the child suffer, but the adults as well. Although more and more couples are divorcing, people never think it will happen to them. With the onset of divorce, couples are ill-prepared for what there is to come. The complexity of separation and forming a new life is new and uncharted for most.[27]

> *The course of the divorce creates not only a power play but also a heightened anger. Anxiety, diminished communication, sadness, conflict, and depression can affect both parties.*

How many of you have been in this position? The end of a marriage, the end of a family unit as you know it, financial fear, and fear of the future. Anyone that has an investment in their family as it was before the discourse would feel some of these, or all of them.

My spouse did not move out, as his attorney advised him not to. I was told not to throw anything away that was his (like his clothes, as this would-be property damage!) However, like many it was not only the clothes I wanted to burn or throw out, it was everything. We had two small children, one nearly two and a three-year-old. It was painful and devastating!

Each of us retained an attorney. Mine was a young kind woman that was too soft, and his was a mean "I don't care asshole." My spouse may not have felt that, but his attorney pushed us further apart on many occasions. No one was looking out to keep the peace, or for there to be harmony, which in turn would have made the transition easier for the children. Working with divorcing couples, I realize that the children are often overlooked. The State has its plan of what you get and how you get it, but what about the children?

It is not the divorce that is the most damaging for the children, but the process by which parents continue to interact after the divorce.

We entered the war zone. Splitting what we had, fighting over custody, and trying not to end up bankrupt from all the fees.

You often wonder when you look back, "How did it come to this? Why did it end up like this?" but in the moment, you must just plan to get through the situation and figure out what is going to be the best for you and the children.

Well, we did get through it and although bruised and defeated at times, it was over.

CHAPTER 5

New Ways to Divorce

· ·

For many of you reading this book the divorce will have been finalized, or you are actively a divorced parent. So, you can skip this chapter

However, for some the step into the divorce arena is just about to begin. This chapter is for you.

Bart Carey Esq., a collaborative attorney, believes divorce can be changed to work for the couple and not the court or attorney. He believes that today, there are other ways to divorce. Rather than the fighting and fear you will be able to use a new way—the Collaborative Divorce. Options are discussed in a collaborative divorce and helpful to move peacefully into the next stage of your life, leaving behind the harshness of the system, a system that needs to be reformed to meet the needs of today's divorcing couples.

Families are forever. Divorce is a transition period. Marriages have communities. Parents have children. Children have grandparents, aunts, uncles, cousins, schools, and communities. It still takes a village.

The way families separate, and divorce, is undergoing a revolutionary change. Divorce can be a client centered approach, not court centered process. The goal of the Client Centered Process is to help parents identify the resources to successfully conclude negotiations for themselves – not to mimic litigation informally.

Driven by the concerns of the spouses to protect their children during the divorce and avoid the financial devastation that too often accompanies a litigated divorce, they are seeking a greater power relative to control over outcomes and a greater voice in the process. A greater ability to define what is and is not important. The Client Centered way better reflects the way families have traditionally *resolved their conflicts* rather than engaged in their conflicts.

The Client Centered ways to divorce provide the support these families seek by designing a process around the client's priorities, supporting and transforming communications focused on solving the problem, and transforming the conflict from "me v. you" to "us" and "our" with the children at the center of a planning process v. pawns in the middle of the fight.

In all his years Carey says, no one has come into his office and said, *'My marriage is falling apart. I don't trust my spouse. We don't agree on anything. We argue all the time. My kids are falling apart at school and home. I am spending more time at the office and I'm less productive. My employer is not happy with me. I'm stressed at home; I'm stressed at work. The stress is killing me. . . . [Long Pause] . . . Tell me what you can do to prolong this grief, fuel the conflict, further scar the kids, and spend all the equity in our home or our children's college savings or both?'*

What they really ask is, *"Help! What is going to happen? How do we stop the fight! How do we stop the chaos! How do I protect my children and get my life back!"* They are done with the fight and want to solve the problem once and for all.

They want peace.

The adversarial nature of litigation is like wet on water. There is no such thing as a 'friendly' litigation. There are many settlement-oriented attorneys. But the context is still adversarial, my rights and entitlements under the law v. yours. Every settlement discussion will be restrained by expected trial outcomes, which can be very difficult to project. [If you ever want to test the certainty of an attorney's projection of your trial outcomes just ask the attorney to bet their fees against it.]

Client Centered divorce allows the following for the couple:

Control of Costs.

Control of Schedules.

Control of Process values:

Length of process

Pace of process

Confidentiality of information

Limited Scope of professional's work

Neutrality of Professionals

How does this Collaborative Divorce Process work?

Let's start with family goals. Newlyweds, at the time they marry, have been making plans. Family plans, career plans and so forth. Now they are wedding their futures together. They are full of love and hopes. They have goals. They had, if you will, a shared mission.

For however long they are married, whether they have children or not or how many, they never, ever, answer a question about how to attain their future goals as a family by reference to the Family Code or local statutes. No one, ever, until conflict rises to the point they are thinking about separation and/or divorce starts asking questions about what the law says. And most of the time they want to know what the law says will happen if they go through a court divorce.

If not the law, what did they use as a planning guide? Their shared mission. Their goals, their unique family values, and common interests. How did they resolve the challenges and solve the problems life presented to them as a family? By finding the best option available to them that best reflected and advanced their shared mission. As long as they shared that mission, they were able to soldier through adversity and meet challenges together. This is the 'heroic' history every couple shares.

But now they find themselves at odds with each other. Trust is broken and suspicions reign. Communication has eroded leading to misunderstandings and, ultimately the breakdown of the marital relationship. They don't believe they can solve this problem by themselves. They feel like adversaries. And they walk into an attorney's office and present the 'new' narrative [e.g., tales of drunkenness and cruelty, in the lyrics of the Kinks song], their failures and the saga of things gone wrong, as we have encapsulated, above.

However, they still can resolve their conflict on their own terms if they have the professional support, education, and information they lack to do so.

Every divorce is a legal process which is 80% emotional and a financial problem to solve.

The three primary domains of divorce are the legal complexities, the financial complexities and the emotional complexities. The couple can navigate and resolve their divorce given the necessary advice, counsel, and support in these three domains. This work is undertaken by an experienced qualified professional 'team'. The couple works directly with their chosen professionals in each area, utilizing the professional best suited for the tasks necessary to complete. For example, they work with the financial professional on developing a financial plan for the future that 'makes all boats float' and leaves no one behind. They work on co-parenting plans with qualified and experienced counselors with family systems training and experience with families transitioning through divorce. And they receive assistance, advice and counsel from experienced family law attorneys.

Emotional Complexities.

While the divorce process is thought of as a legal process, it is 80% emotional. It wasn't an argument about the law that led to the breakdown of the marriage. It was the breakdown of what I call the Holy Trinity of interpersonal relationships. Trust, Relationship, and Communications are the Trinity. For convenience we will refer to these 3 collectively as the Trinity hereafter.

A breakdown in any one of the Trinity leads to the erosion in the others and the erosion of anyone leads to the eventual breakdown in the others. Families develop complex systems to function. In a divorce, these family systems, which have been breaking down, necessarily must give way to a new, more functional family system to reflect the new configuration of the family. In order to help families, understand how to restructure into a new family system and improve their participation in their new roles as parents but not marital partners, for instance, mental health professionals are brought in as a part of the 'team'. They serve to educate the parents and teach new skills and tools for co-parenting communications and cooperation. They are called "Coaches" due to the resemblance of their work duties to athletic coaches. Teach the fundamentals and practice new skills.

Financial Complexities.

One of the best Collaborative Coaches I know says he has observed that the average person is more likely to share intimate details of their sex life than the intimate details of their finances. I am no longer surprised at the couple that reports they have never had a budget before and one of them has exclusively handled the finances.

It's well known that many couples argue and fight over their finances. Reasons vary, but finances are often the proxy war for the underlying tensions that belie the ways in which the Trinity have broken down. For instance, it is common for one spouse to be mostly unaware of the details of the couple's marital estate. This may not have been an issue while communications and trust were high for the couple. But if trust, for instance, begins to erode and affects communications, financial communications may break down. Lacking trust and information arguments break out, further damaging trust and relationship. If the couple cannot reverse the trend, pretty soon the Trinity becomes an irretrievable casualty of the formerly agreeable arrangement.

Warranted or not, suspicions of self-dealing, control and breaches of fiduciary duties arise.

In order to restore confidence and trust by both spouses that they know and understand their finances at this critical time, the 'team' includes one, neutral Collaborative Financial Analysts, with credentials like CFP, CPA and CDFA, gather all the financial information and compile reports detailing the marital estate, the cash flow, and the needs of each spouse as they transition from one household to two. The neutrality of the Collaborative Financial Analyst is to assure the clients of their objectivity and impartiality in completing their work. These Collaborative Financial Analysts educate the 'team', and particularly the less knowledgeable spouse, and answer all the financial questions. The couple will use the information, with the support of the 'team', to build two post marital estates and budget for two households and the children's needs.

Legal Complexities.

They can have sound legal advice and support from attorneys who will sign a Stipulation and Order that they will never take the case to court. This last piece is known as the "disqualification clause". It limits the scope of the attorney's work and aligns with the client's desire to settle out of court. Otherwise, without the limitation on the scope of the legal work, the attorney's professional and ethical duty is to make sure the client and the case is well positioned and prepared for the eventual trial. This means controlling the information, timing, and limiting settlement options to those most likely to be defensible at trial, if there were one. As mentioned before, these may conform to the Family Code but bear little relationship to the client's goals, values and interests.

It takes two to marry and two to divorce. However, sometimes it does not seem that way; it seems more as if you are on an island alone with no life jacket.

CHAPTER 6

Reconcile with Yourself First

. . . .

A llow yourself to grieve and feel whatever you want. There are no rules about how you should feel; it is all so much about the experience you had in the marriage and the course of its breakdown. However, if you work through understanding your own pain, you will move faster into the next stage of acceptance. Whatever that means - hot baths, screaming in the back garden, staying in bed for a while, exercising excessively- it really does not matter as long as it is not harmful, and is temporary. Normal as you know it is gone! Confusion changes and rearranges your life on so many levels.

This can be difficult but can also be a cathartic experience. Depending on who wanted the divorce, this phase will be different for each of you. Some couples, even in a good breakup (if there is such a thing), feel the loss.

In my case I got angry, then I got angrier. I think we can all attest to feeling this way about certain situations and then in the end we calm down. But in divorce it is final; the feelings need to be worked through while dealing with all the other stuff that life gives us.

Normal as you know it is gone! Confusion changes and rearranges your life on so many levels.

I would spend my day in my head playing over what happened and what I should do next. I was in disbelief, as I was not aware that the divorce was coming, and I was not the one that initiated it by filing. I was in a daze thinking about what I was going to do now. I found an attorney who really was not the right fit, but I felt the urge to do something to protect myself. I took the advice of friends and the people around me. Waiting is not an opportunity that one has when facing a divorce. There is so much to do. I went into a state of shock, then hope, then acceptance.

Figuring out how to manage, parent, and share the children was overwhelming. I could not bear the thought of my children leaving me, even for one day.

You will go through the loss of a dream. We are not talking about abusive relationships when we talk about this phase, as any relationship that has abuse of any kind needs to end. You must accept that the relationship has reached the point of no return and is no longer salvageable. However, even at this stage the foundation for what you need to do to move on is still there and waiting to be used. I believe we all have it in us to bridge the gap between sheer pain and understanding, from shock to acceptance, from hurt to forgiveness.

It takes two to marry and two to divorce. However, sometimes it does not seem that way; it seems more as if you are on an island alone with no life jacket.

Everyone is different when the end of a relationship happens. You might have been the parent that stayed at home and took care of running the home, or you might have been the parent that left every day for work. One of you may never have realized that you were this far along in the demise of the

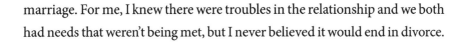

marriage. For me, I knew there were troubles in the relationship and we both had needs that weren't being met, but I never believed it would end in divorce.

> *I believe we all have it in us to bridge the gap between sheer pain and understanding, from shock to acceptance, from hurt to forgiveness.*

I can be honest and say there were times I imagined not being married to my husband, and often wondered what it would be like to be in a marriage that felt like I was loved. However, I do realize today, perhaps most importantly, that we both are the reason the marriage ended. When you own your contribution, positive or negative, to the relationship, it helps with the healing process. It is sad that some divorces could have been avoided, possibly if the right intervention was there.

Today, as a couple's therapist and a specialist in relationships, I realize just what I did wrong, and how I could have changed that situation, if only I had better understood my role within my marriage, and the marriage itself.

We also need to know that we bring our history and past experiences into the relationship. We do not just marry our spouse; we marry their past with their own childhood issues and parenting styles. Hopefully, these can merge but, in many marriages, before a divorce, they have not and are often part of the reason for the breakup.

> *When you own your part of the relationship, it helps with the healing process.*

Be kind to yourself; The more you allow the loss and the pain to be a part of your whole day the longer it will take to work forward and become whole again. We know that even if this is what you want, there is still the loss of a dream and the end of an era. If you are to move on, then all the pieces must be put back into a new puzzle that is now yours. I call this THE NEW FAMILY.

What that looks like is up to you; there will be changes in every area of your life—finances, parenting, social life, sex life, and general lifestyle. For many, this might be parallel and for others a dramatic change, no matter what that new family looks like. You will need to find your homeostasis for your world to stop rocking so it is important to allow yourself time before you work on making your world stable again.

We bring our history and past into the relationship.

ANGER, SHAME, AND GUILT

These three bedfellows are a big part of the end of a relationship, and often felt by both members and at different times.

Many people do not understand what anger is, but if they understood what is behind anger, then it would be easier to let go of it. Anger is linked to a perception of damage or hurt and can often come from a feeling of unfairness and the feeling of expectations not met. Unfairness is often a strong feeling in divorce and must be worked out by looking at what you are in control of. You are ultimately entirely in control of your emotions- you decide how angry you wish to be. Keeping unfairness at the forefront of your mind will only hold you hostage to the pain of ANGER. It is not easy, as unfairness is a very powerful feeling!

Many people do not understand what anger is, but if they understood what is behind anger, then it would be easier to let go of anger.

I believe SHAME AND GUILT are easier to tackle than anger seems to be! Shame comes from the feeling that we have done something wrong. This leaves us with a feeling that we are flawed. When we feel flawed it comes in a package with feeling inadequate and bad about ourselves. Divorce is not what anyone wants really; the outcome of shame is feeling less-than, which does nothing to build the situation that you need to build—a harmonious relationship for co-parenting.

Guilt is associated with doing something wrong. If you are leaving a marriage that you believed would be there forever, then feeling guilty is connected to that mindset. It is important to look towards the future and how you can invest in building a new relationship with your partner without feeling that you have done something wrong.

There is the negative voice in your head that consists of blaming yourself or of shame that others will judge you. No matter how many divorces or if you come from divorced parents yourself, it is still an end of an era and one that often shame is attached to. As we process, we can choose to allow the inner story with its illogical views to control us or take action to move into our new life.

If you are leaving a marriage that you believed would be there forever, then feeling guilty is connected to that mindset.

CHAPTER 7

Anxiety, Co-Parenting, and Mindfulness

. . . .

Anxiety is a condition that many people experience. However, when going through a divorce, anxiety might be present for the first time. The symptoms include tension, increased heart rate, sweaty palms, light-headedness, difficulty breathing, tension, flush feelings.

These are often symptoms that can be confused with other conditions like heart attacks, stomach flus, insomnia, lethargy, or even just fear. Anxiety not only affects how you feel but also affects behavior—not wanting to be in certain situations, trying to control events, and often leaving situations when anxiety occurs.

The command your body is giving you during an anxiety attack is: "fight, flight or freeze."

These responses are there to protect us when we are in danger. An example would be when you are in your car and it breaks down. It is 3A.M. and your phone is dead. You have to get out of the car, and you realize you are in a very dangerous area. As you walk to find a place where you can make a call, you hear voices behind you and it now feels dangerous. You have a choice to run, find a place to hide, or prepare to fight.

In this situation, we are grateful that we have this trigger to protect ourselves. However, the feeling of anxiety does not contain itself to a dangerous situation and rears its ugly head at times when we don't need any of these responses.

The command your body is giving you during an anxiety attack is: "fight, flight or freeze."

During a divorce, there are many times parents revert to "fight, flight or freeze". A one-on-one argument with the former partner would be an example of the Fight response. Flight can be seen in avoiding the partner, and the tough discussions necessary to moving forward. In some cases, individuals can freeze by stopping the discussions, and not moving forward with reconciliation. There is a perception of threat for the person's safety, financially and emotionally. There is a sense of vulnerability and over responding to a perceived danger. Divorce creates the what-ifs and there are many. What-ifs are triggers to set up a situation as unsafe. How do you contain the anxiety and fear?

One of the ways is with MINDFULNESS

As explained in Dr. Diane Gehart's Book *Mindfulness for Chocolate Lovers*, mindfulness has three elements:

1. Self-regulated awareness in something that is a physical or emotional experience occurring in the present and being able to focus the mind intently.
2. Making non-judgmental observations.
3. Accepting "what is" with compassion.

Life is so full of "stuff." Whether it is putting the laundry in the dryer, taking a bunch of old clothes to the thrift shop, or making dinner, it seems hard to believe you could stop long enough to use mindfulness. However, we are programmed to believe that we must be productive and if stopping to take care of ourselves is not productive in the societal understanding of the word "PRODUCTIVE," then we must reevaluate what we want to feel. I believe after the rocky road of divorce, most want to feel safe, relaxed, and able to move on peacefully—in the present.

If you take care of your mind, it is a start.

To be mindful, you need more than just stopping in the moment.

First and foremost, you need to focus. This is not to be confused with just taking your mind off work, watching TV, or sitting in the sun; this is about concentration with no other distraction.

Second, you need to be receptive to co-parenting and what your life is now made up of. Being able to be with what is, no matter if it is unpleasant, or something you want to avoid.

As I often tell my patients in the office, anxiety cannot exist in the present, only in the fear of the past or the fear of the future. During mindfulness you are fully present, you are one with the very moment you are in.

In addition, to being present, you need to be aware of being judgmental. It is easy to let our minds go to judgments, even when we don't want to. We are programmed to judge, or we would not look before we crossed a road.[11]

In mindfulness, we need to be aware of unhealthy judgments trying to get into our mind, and work to move these judgments aside.

Finally, be kind and gentle with yourself. While trying to be mindful, you might feel like you're not getting it! Or you might be frustrated with yourself. It can be difficult to focus, but learning these steps is an important part of moving into a state of mindfulness.

Anxiety cannot exist in the present, only in the fear of the past or the fear of the future.

CHAPTER 8

My Journey Dealing with the End of the Dream

· ·

In my relationship, I was not waiting for divorce or the breakdown of my family unit. I was not happy at times, but not ready for divorce. My former husband felt differently and filed for divorce. It was unexpected but looking back it should not have been. I was in shock and very angry. However, it takes two to marry and two to divorce.

It was a difficult time, not only because I was hurt and angry but also because my spouse was the one that filed; it seemed so cold and callous. But at the end of a marriage, it becomes all about the legal side of a relationship.

I wanted to understand, deal with the shock, and find some way to cope with what was going to happen. However, when you are the one that is served or the hurt party, it is hard to see through the fog. My spouse went about his day, but today I know it was not easy for him either.

His attorney told him to stay in the house and to expect me to behave as if it was home life as usual; good luck on that one! I wanted to throw his clothes out, smash his stuff, and scream at him 24/7. BUT THIS WAS NOT TO BE!

Once the attorney is involved, the focus is getting the most for the client. Most care more about this, no matter the damage it does to the future relationship of the couple. Attorneys leave the scene when the last signature is signed and leave in their wake a tornado of pain, grief, anger, shock, and frustration! It was hard to be in the same house with my spouse after the filing but may have been a blessing. We had to learn to live within close proximity for the duration of the divorce process.

It is hard in the beginning of a divorce to see your role, but the sooner you understand your role the better it will be for the children. We feel we must fight to survive and use the many defense mechanisms that are there to protect our very being. Those involved are shell-shocked.

For me, it was nearly a year after the divorce when I had truly reconciled. After the dust had settled, we were able to build a bridge and create a co-parenting environment that did not consist of discourse and anger.

However, this does not happen overnight. There is a lot of work to do to get to this point, and both spouses must be ready to reframe their relationship into one that works for the children.

I know this firsthand, not only from my own experience but from working with so many that are divorcing. There is denial and misunderstanding in the early stages that tends to hinder the bridge to co-parenting. I have been told by many couples that they could not do this; the pain and anger are too deep. But I beg to differ; I believe with the right understanding, the therapeutic intervention of the right kind, a softer and less aggressive divorce, all can successfully co-parent in the end.

After the dust had settled, we were able to build a bridge and create a co-parenting environment that did not consist of discourse and anger. However, it did not happen overnight.

The kids in our life do not ask for this; we must love our children more than we hate our spouse.

Not all spouses will be able to do this, but with help, I believe more can. We are led to believe we must dislike each other when a divorce occurs, not to speak kindly to each other, and to think badly of one another because of the hurt.

What we forget is this is the person we fell in love with, the person that we believed would be there for the rest of our life and is the father or mother of our children. WE MUST DO THE RIGHT THING FOR THE CHILDREN!

CHAPTER 9

Pain, Pain And More Pain

. . . .

In this chapter, we will look at the overall pain of divorce—a relationship over, a lost love, guilt and shame, and a fractured family. It is universal pain, and no one gets away scot-free even if you want the divorce. There is real pain from having to manage your new way of life and then there is that voice in your head that just keeps pushing the buttons of anger. This negative talk adds fuel to the fire already in your life and only prolongs growing and moving forward. What you do know is that it is over, and the sooner the weeds are pulled, and the new plants grow in, the faster life will return to what you want it to be.

> *It is universal pain, and no one gets away scot-free even if you want the divorce.*

The love that we have lost is not to be marginalized.

There are stages of grief that a person goes through when someone dies. However, even if the person you are leaving is not dead, the feelings often are similar. There is anger, a sense of who is to blame.

The blame game often keeps us away from family and friends to avoid reliving the hurt. Although hard, there needs to be honest self-reflection on our part of the discourse, and what we contribute to the conversation. There may be very little happiness in your world right now but hold on to the future; it can only get brighter.

Different situations cause a couple to divorce. For example, co-parenting difficulties, adultery, finances, addiction. When a family has fallen apart based on any of these, the pain can be all-consuming. There is a level of suffering with these conditions that adds to the grief of divorce and makes it harder not to feel a sense of depression or greater loss.

How many years you were married and how many years in the divorce process is not really an issue. Your dreams of the future were still about the two of you. Divorce shatters those dreams and leaves you in a place of helplessness. At times it will feel as if you have been stretched beyond the fray, not just physically but also mentally and financially. The pain will go eventually, and you will be on the other side. If you take all the steps to grow and build a better union between you and the other person that was in the marriage, you will be able to see a brighter future.

Divorce shatters those dreams and leaves you in a place of helplessness.

The freedom that you want from your union comes with an enormous price, but what doesn't?

The family unit as you knew it is changed forever, but a new one needs to be developed. The family that may have looked like the perfect family will be forced to admit to society they were not the perfect family after all. Families must accept they are not perfect and are forced to come to terms with the loss of an image.

*The pain will go eventually, and
you will be on the other side.*

The family becomes fractured and at this time the parents are often focused on finding another partner for comfort and to not be alone. What parents seem to lose sight of at this time in the divorce is they are not alone, there are children that need them the most. This can often cause conflict with trying to balance a new relationship with the old relationship with the spouse. A 2012 study reported that the presence of post separation conflict and in some cases triangulation of the child, can cause parental alienation. Alienation often leads to problems internally and externally for the child and research shows that often a child in adulthood, has an identity crisis.[12]

*The family unit as you knew it is changed
forever, but a new one needs to be developed.*

CHAPTER 10

New Partner Jealousy

. . . .

If we are to address this issue, we must look at everyone's role in the problem. The idea of effectively co-parenting as the new family is not a typical way to behave, as the general masses expect you to be angry at each other. Due to the anger, communication skills often are lacking, and parents will communicate through a parent app, which is often required by the court system. This parenting app is a method of communication between partners that the courts have access to. This encourages respectful and less volatile communication these curt emails or texts leave much to be deciphered, and the animosity and hurt grows. The difficulty for the children at this time, and the legacy that is given to them, is unfair. No child is born into our lives to be used as a pawn or to be used as a co-conspirator in a damaged relationship.

I KNOW you can effectively co-parent; I have done it! Moving into a better place is possible in co-parenting, but again it will not happen overnight or without effort from both sides.

. . . .

Children need you more than you know and although you want a new life with a new person it cannot be at the expense of the children.

. . . .

One of the most difficult situations is when one or both partners enter a new relationship. What we have found is in some cases the arrangement works. However, in so many relationships there is the element of jealousy, fear, and a lack of trust. Hopefully, a person works on themselves before they enter another relationship, but often that does not happen. Although many want to be with someone rather than be alone, and if the effort was on understanding yourself first, it would be better for the future of the children.

Relationships end for a reason and it is important to work on these issues as you move forward.

One of the things to remember when you are starting a new relationship is the home your children are in with you. **THIS IS THEIR HOME,** their safe place. It must be made a haven and not a place where they are visitors. In many new relationships there is jealousy of the children – a new partner may treat children as if they are guests within their own home, which can feel very alienating and destabilizing. It is amazing how many don't see this in the new relationship but assume the children are making waves or being jealous themselves.

It must be made a haven and not a place where they are visitors.

Well, one thing we know is that the children came first and must be first no matter what. This might seem hard, but they did not choose to be born nor did they choose for you to end a family system. Children need you more than you know and although you want a new life with a new person it cannot be at the expense of the children.

For many, there is the presence of **TERRITORIALIZING**. Many may not know this word, but it CAN BE the major player for incoming new partners. It seems important for incoming partners to make their mark, HENCE TERRITORIALIZING.

This does not happen with all new partners, but unfortunately, the ones that don't want to share the parent with the children have a need to territorialize. However, it is for the parent to be aware of this situation and open their eyes WIDE to see the signs.

An example of territorializing is when a new partner comes over to the parents' house at times where it should just be the children, leaving the children feeling less important, and the new partner feeling empowered. Other times a new partner will require attention when a child has a need, and the parent must choose between the new partner or his/her children. Invariably the children pay!

The new partner wins. Why, might you ask? Because the parent could lose the new partner if they don't do what the new partner wants, and often believe that they cannot lose their children. THE CHILDREN are not going anywhere but they are in fact moving further away from their relationship with the parent. The children are going to feel unimportant and second to the new partner. You see, for a parent that is trying to build a new relationship when the children are around, it must be a collaborative arrangement. The children's feelings must be taken into consideration.

One of the many comments I hear from parents is that the children just want to control me, the children don't want me to spend time with this person, the children are making it hard This happens because they are suffering from the divorce. It might seem like they are making life difficult, and they might be, but remember you are the parent that set this up.

> ### The children's feelings must be taken into consideration.

49

Doing things, the right way can only be a plus. Jumping into a new relationship often comes with fallout and you will have to be aware of how to make it work.

The **<u>NEW FAMILY</u>** also must have time together; this is not uncommon when you have children. There are meetings at the school, sport meets, music performances. These are off times when the jealous new partner feels the most vulnerable and often makes the situation difficult for the children and the family. Remember at this time, WHO IS THE ADULT?

It might seem like they are making life difficult, and they might be, but remember you are the parent that set this up.

CHAPTER 11

Parentification: What it Looks Like and How it Hurts!

. . . .

Ivan Boszormeny-Nagy, the Hungarian-American psychiatrist, one of the founders of the field of **family therapy,** used the word parentification to describe what happens in a family when the child and parent roles are switched.[16]

It is not uncommon for this to happen after a divorce. Children are used for emotional support and become the delivery service between the two parents. Children should never become a parent's support system. The role of the parent is to be the provider. Parental guidance and protection are needed for a child's sense of safety. A parentified child is forced to take on responsibilities that are not theirs to take. The process of parent-child relationships gets turned around. The parent is unable to be a solid role model. Often this role, once established, is hard to break and has far-reaching effects on the stability of the mental and physical health of the child. The child is expected to help with the family housework and babysitting beyond what would be age appropriate.[16]

A parentified child is forced to take on responsibilities that are not theirs to take.

There are many reasons a parent parentified the child. Parentification is the parent treating the child as if they were an adult, with all the expectations that come along with that. These children have no one to look to and grow up too fast. Often the child leaves behind the childhood that they are owed and grow up to have a greater sense of responsibility than is appropriate. These children are affected for the rest of their lives. They become overly responsible in close relationships and want to rescue people from their pain. Often attracted to partners that need saving, it leaves them burdened to a life of hard work emotionally and physically.

In substance abusive parents, they were often the victim of their own abuse, or issues in childhood. The children of these parents have an impossible task of making their parents feel better. Not only are they parentified but they also become parentless when the parent is under the influence of drugs. Parents with drug and alcohol addiction create a situation where the children worry about the safety of the parent. Not knowing what might happen to a drunk parent, children become hyper vigil and protective.[16]

There are two different types of parentification: Instrumental and Emotional.

Instrumental Parentification

In instrumental parentification, children become responsible for taking care of the siblings, grandparents, or any relative that the parent is responsible for. These children often make their own meals and become accountable for household duties. It is not uncommon for these children to become cooks and even shoppers! In families where the parent does not speak the primary language, the child becomes the translator and often the bill payer.[16]

Emotional parentification

Emotional parentification is all about feelings. The child becomes the conduit of the parent's feelings. They become the parent's vessel of survival.

> *Parents will tell a child that they are now the man or woman of the house, putting pressure on the child to fill a role they should not have.*

Children are roped into becoming the person the parent wants to share their problems with. It is not uncommon for the parent to ask the child for advice or to evaluate a situation. The children are asked to mediate between the parents and/or family members. They are often told secrets and made to keep these secrets from the other parent. A parent might break down emotionally and expect comfort from the child. Children that play this role live in confusion. They have two dilemmas; they cannot fix their parents and the other is they give up the time to develop a sense of self. The children become parents to their parents, losing that parental unit in their lives. Parents will tell a child that they are now the man or woman of the house, and this puts pressure on the child to fill a role they should not have.[16]

> *The children become parents to their parents, losing that parental unit in their lives.*

As the child becomes the parent to the siblings, they become more than just a helper. They become their sibling's confidante, adviser, and comforter. This is a sad situation and sad for the child. Often the parentified child has no one to look up to, as they feel they are the grown-up. These children are often weighed down with responsibilities and grow up way too fast. By growing up too fast, these children have had to develop empathy and understanding for others, leaving out the right they have as children to be selfish at times. It is a violation of boundaries and is one of the factors in unhealthy adult relationships.

Healthy Instrumental/ Emotional Parenting

Not all interactions are bad when they are age-appropriate, and they can often build a child up. When a child needs to have a situation explained, such as a parent being upset or sad, the child should receive clarity. This helps build the child's understanding rather than the child becoming a fixer.[16]

Helping around the house when there is a single-parent household is not inappropriate. Children can gain a sense of pride and satisfaction in helping around the house. It gives the child a sense of competence. This being said, helping out should not be at the expense of the child's emotional or physical health. The children in single-parent homes still need to have time for themselves. Helping should not replace the time they need to do schoolwork, peer relationships, or just be kids.[16]

CHAPTER 12

Therapy after the Filing of Divorce

· ·

I believe that therapy should be a major player in the process at the end of a marriage. I decided to go into therapy to work on being the best mother I could because I did not want to damage my children because of my anger.

It was a difficult time and an end of a dream for both of us. No one goes into a marriage waiting for the end, but they must pick up the pieces even if they were the one to file. Therapy helps take some of the sting out of the end.

By seeing your role and the difficulties in the marriage, it is possible with a good therapist to work on honesty. It is not uncommon to blame the other person for the end of the marriage. However, by seeing the issues that were in the relationship and the issues that you each had, it is possible to remove the personal feelings from the situation.

Finding a therapist that works for you is important; not all therapists are right for everyone. It is not a bad thing to change therapists if it seems to be a bad fit. I know working with so many couples over the years that there are different needs with different personalities. I remember the first therapist that I went to. She began by calling my spouse a narcissistic male and pathological (mentally ill), which for me was not true, but these remarks made me feel angry at her!

We have our own names and feelings for the spouse at the end of a marriage; we don't need others providing us with more negative feelings, especially when we have gone for help. What is needed for a therapist at this time is to sit with you wherever you are in the process, not to rush you to the finish line and not to pathologize your ex-partner.

Therapy helps take some of the sting out of the end. Finding a therapist that works for you is important; not all therapists are right for everyone.

As you work through the divorce, the therapist will be able to ground you in reality. The world does not stand still while you process working on the loss and changes. In addition, the therapist will allow you to have a neutral ear and opinion that will be different than family members and friends. It is good at this time to find a therapist that has experience with divorce and the difficulties that are involved with the journey and children.

Many U.S. states require divorcing parents to take education classes about the impact of divorce on parents and children.

During my therapy, I wanted answers to "Why?" But that was not my reason to enter therapy. I wanted to grow and be a better parent. However, the therapist that I first went to was all about finding fault with my former spouse. The next therapist just sat and listened, but I wanted responses. The third went straight to the heart of my hurt and loss. She told me that it took 2 and that I was a party to the breakup (not something I wanted to hear) and that I could choose to be the best parent I wanted to be. She was good! I learned if I didn't end my own pain and accept my role, I would not grow; I needed to grow.

Custody Battles and Divorce

Custody battles play a major role in the disruption of cooperative co-parenting. The parental role is defined by the interactions that occur throughout the divorce process. The lack of a structural role definition leaves the parents to construct their own. When both spouses have an amicable experience during the divorce interactions, they can form a shared understanding of the definition of parental roles.

When there are no shared parental definitions at the beginning of the divorce stage, the parental role is ambiguous, negative, and often impacts the long-term parental roles. Post-divorce litigation is often present when cooperative parenting custody has not been established early. When mothers and fathers overestimate the other parent's level of custody satisfaction, the issue of dissatisfaction is not acknowledged and creates an increased conflict over parenting issues.[14]

In my relationship, the divorce could not be finalized, as the custody battle was ongoing and left us both with a bad taste for each other. The main issue was time, we both wanted more. In some ways, lucky kids that they had such caring parents. But in some battles, it is about cost and paying less child support.

> *When there are no shared parental definitions at the divorce stage, the parental role is ambiguous, negative and often impacts the long-term parental roles.*

A research study found four conditions must exist for cooperative co-parenting:

1. Both spouses despite differences must be able to agree to communicate about parenting, support each other, and make flexible arrange-

ments. An agreement must be established in respect to rules for parenting and co-parenting schedules, details, and lifestyles. In addition, custody agreements need to be initiated by the parents and should not be left up to the courts.

Children need to have love from their parents. Co-parents may have different lifestyles, but the stabilizing factor must be that the children know they have two strong advocates that trust each other when it comes to the care and parenting of the child.

2. Geographic proximity is an important factor. In an ideal cooperative arrangement, access is important; parents need to be present.
3. Children need to be involved and although it cannot always be a 100 percent the way they want it, they must be included.
4. Discussions that deal with issues that do not pertain to the wellbeing of the child should be dealt with only in the parents' presence.[9]

Being able to change a date for the other parent to fulfill an appointment or family function shows love for the child, not a sense of being manipulated by the former partner.

There needs to be an establishment of the new order. The Ernst and Altis's[9] study acknowledged this idea in stating that although there are different homes the parents and the children are still a "family". Cooperative co-parenting can help the child learn to reduce sexism by seeing both parents carry out similar roles and share responsibility.

The authors believe co-parenting is a parenting style, not just a 'pick-up the pieces' alternative. Parents are taking on both roles, and often roles they had never been a party to. For many, taking on all the roles needed in a family is tough and can be overwhelming, but this is often the first time many realize how much work it takes!

The world of custody is often perceived differently by both parents. For them, there is no prior experience and no socially prescribed norms. Not only do parents have to redefine their parental role, but also their marital role. In a 2002 study[22] mothers reported a higher level of conflict over parenting issues than the fathers. The level of involvement was perceived differently. It is not uncommon for each parent to see the other's role from their own lens.

Mothers often see fathers as being less involved, and fathers often perceive themselves as being more involved. In the area of skills, fathers felt satisfaction in their ability to parent. It is an adjustment period and a time to evaluate how you can change your view and expectation. I believe children adapt in these times. If at dad's home they have more spaghetti dinners, it is not something that is wrong or inadequate parenting, but what it is like at dads.

For mothers, it is often important for the situation at dads to reflect their own, but the family is now different and in **The New Family** there are new and different systems in place when it comes to care in the home. It is sad in some ways, as the ideal situation is for a child to be in a single home, a truth that children adapt to. Parents need to adapt too.

This was a tough time for me, as I was so involved in the children's program at home—what they ate, what they wore, what they watched on TV. I only gave them organic food! Now they were eating and drinking whatever their dad gave them during his time with them. It was a hard adjustment, but in the big picture did it really matter on those days. Once I let go and stopped buying the organic milk and sending it over, I was free to let them be a family on their time. We get to do things on our time and on our conditions. Pretty exciting each parent might have ideas that they never explored as a couple and now can make decisions no matter how small. Maybe you want a vegan household or a gluten free household!

Studies have shown both parents report reluctance for visitation changes.

Fathers perceived mothers to be less willing and accommodating when it came to changing plans. However, mothers perceived themselves as being more willing to change than their former spouse. The authors found these disagreements interfered with the ability to establish a cooperative co-parenting relationship.[22]

In my relationship, I had the same difficulties that many couples experience. We had set days and weekends which had been worked out by the court system and the attorneys who really had no investment in our children's future. After the final signing, our life and custody were of no interest to them. Hence, as divorcing couples, we must work through what we need as a family, not what the court has ordered, or our attorneys have fought for. The court orders a cookie-cutter plan, but not all plans fit all couples or all families.

Being able to change a date for the other parent to fulfill an appointment or family function shows love for the child, not a sense of being manipulated by the former partner. Parents that can do this early in the new co-parenting relationship will set a precedent for a healthier and happier situation.

As divorcing couples, we must work through what we need as a family, not what the court has ordered, or our attorneys have fought for.

CHAPTER 13

Fathers' Parenting Role in Divorce

· ·

For many fathers, this is the first time they have taken on the role as parent alone, and for mothers the first time they have not been able to oversee their child. Both of these are new norms for parents; hence, parents need to focus on establishing a well-defined cooperative parenting plan.

With the establishment of the school year, holidays, vacations, birthdays, parental transportation, and agreement on methods for dispute resolution, a mother's struggle with relinquishing parental control will be diminished. It is not easy for any parent to leave their child. However, a father has to take on the role of both parents, so it is not easy for the father. In this newly established custody, it gives the mother time to redefine her parental role and focus on the meaning of her own life post-divorce.

We know post-divorce a father's access to their child is often diminished and the influence they have over their children changes. This situation often leaves the father feeling disenfranchised from their parental role. A mother who is not satisfied with the father's parenting will instigate the use of "gatekeeper". A gatekeeper is an individual that makes all the decisions for the child's schedule. This strategy minimizes the time the child has with their father and creates discord and conflict.[22]

However, current research shows many fathers wish to parent with a gender equal fatherhood approach. This model has become more common in the cultural and social structures of everyday life and in the ways in which people think of possible post-divorce custody solutions. Thankfully this approach increases the bond children can develop with their fathers.[3]

> *Post-divorce, a father's access to their child is often diminished and the influence they have over their children changes.*

Children need both parents. There is not one that is more needed than the other. The need for control often plays a role in how much exposure the children have to each parent- a very sad situation indeed.

There are studies that show that dads can become "Disney Dads."[26] Fathers are often seen as the parent that played more – more physical and less intimate – while the mother gave the emotional support to the child.[28]

This is a situation I often see when working with children of divorce. Often the children will report that they do playful things with Dad and Mom is more about anxiety. The authors suggest that this is the new father role, one that has moved beyond the traditional role of breadwinner and disciplinarian. The father's role is changing and the gap between men and women's participation is shrinking, hence the role the man perceived as a parent in the new relationship is changing.

Many fathers fight for more time and work to make space in their single life for the child.

For a mother, there is still the sense that a child needs the mother's role. Fathers today are looking at the role they need to play differently when divorced. It is no longer a single role, but today fathers' function on multiple levels of parenting.

Arditti and Kelly[4] analyzed the father's perspective of cooperative co-parenting from a system's framework. The authors found fathers valued the custody arrangements the most, and the custody affected the quality of their co-parenting. The more satisfied the father was with the custody arrangements, the more likely he was to have a friendly relationship and a better cooperative co-parenting arrangement.

Many weekend fathers do want more time with their children, but work schedules and lower income can often make it infeasible for their children to live with them. For others the legal battle is too costly. In a study based on 1030 young adults whose parents had divorced before they were sixteen, the present quality of their relationship was highly correlated with the days they lived with their fathers. The more days they had lived with their father the better their adult relationship was. Children that had lived with their father 35% to 50% reported a better relationship. However, above 50% there was no real change in the correlation. In this same study 80 students who lived in dual residences reported that this was a great plan, and years after the divorce had a strong bond with both parents. In contrast over half of the children that lived with just their mother and spent very little time with their father, reported being unhappy about the loss. This group also reported that their relationship with their father had ended.[24]

The second issue for the father was the number of topics the former spouse wanted to discuss. The co-parenting satisfaction for the father was better when the topics were wider in scope and a mix of parental and nonparental topics, and without criticism and shaming. It is hard in a divorced situation at times to keep the conversation always on the issues.

No one is perfect and hurtful topics slip in. Practice will help if you are aware of what it does to the relationship, and in time the need to lecture or share will diminish.[4]

With better conversations and ones that are based around the children, such as the fathers being included more in decision making and being given the option to give their own opinion, fathers reported a closer relationship with their children and had more of a positive opinion of their former spouse. In addition, when the fathers took more responsibility for the end of the marriage, the better the relationship with the spouse became, along with an increase in amicable conversations. Remember, it takes two to marry and two to divorce. Cooperation and sharing information about family issues will improve the co-parenting arena.[4]

Studies have also reported the effects of parenting programs with fathers. The report showed a decrease in childhood disruptive behavior after a father had completed a program.[25]

Fathers with higher education and fewer children reported friendly and more cooperative relationships. The correlation to poor father involvement before the divorce did not predict less involvement after divorce; the opposite was true.[4] Fathers in general today take on the role with a deeper sense of reasonability. Many fathers do not stop at the traditional role of a mother versus father. Fathers have become more involved in their children's emotional needs, not just their physical needs.

For fathers a high-conflict divorce can be seen as a biographical reality, rather than a dilemma. Parents taking a stand, engaging in, and staying with, the issues that eventually result in them being labelled as high-conflict couples is not always true. Actively engaging in the relationship can also be part of the relationship even with some tension.[25] Many children felt it was a hassle to travel between two homes but the benefits of seeing both their father and mother outweighed the inconvenience. Children that got the weekend with their fathers that were younger felt less inconvenienced, and teenagers who tended to have more social lives felt more inconvenienced. However, they all preferred living with both parents than only one. The children that got to spend time with their dad and their mom appreciated the importance of close relationships.[24]

My spouse's role changed. He now had to figure out where they would live as this new family and what his role was going to be. As a mother, it was hard for me to let go. Even though I know the court had ordered days for the children to be with their dad, it was painful. I am sure many of you reading this can attest to those first few weeks or months.

I felt they were too young to leave me, and like all mothers that are invested in their children, believed it was my role and place to take care of all their needs.

Mothering is not a chore but an innate sense of attachment. I believe this is one of the hardest areas of the divorce and looking back it was for their father too. In the beginning, I did not think this way, it was his choice to divorce, and now my role was to not have my children and to see them leave. How this is handled is crucial for the child; this can set in motion a deep sense of loss for the child. It is important to start to build an understanding of what is going to happen in the future. This is where many of us suffer from both parents. As parents that love their children, it is understandable, we don't want to experience a loss either. We are dealing with many changes at the same time and this one can be the most difficult.

CHAPTER 14

Divorce and Gender Roles in Parenting

. . . .

Gender role differences in co-parenting found that different genders often had different yardsticks for measuring the relationship. One of the most significant was the relationship between forgiveness and remorse, and its relationship to cooperative co-parenting.[6]

Forgiveness and remorse play a larger role for the mother, and when acknowledgment and regret is expressed by the father it increases effective co-parenting. Fathers tend to be more aware of external situations for the end of the marriage, and view forgiveness and accountability as unimportant factors. However, forgiveness and remorse are important to mothers because they often feel more hostility at the end of the relationship.

For women, the acknowledgment and regret expressed by their former spouse was crucial to effectively co-parent.

Forgiveness is a therapeutic intervention for cooperative co-parenting. The pain of divorce is similar to other psychological traumas seen in the therapeutic room, which makes forgiveness not easy. When you have been the scorned party, it seems impossible. However, individuals must examine their role in the breakup and how they can own some of the responsibility for the end of the union. If this is questioned, then the possibility for forgiveness will be easier.

With forgiveness, you forgive your spouse, and release yourself from your own prison cell of anger. Forgiveness gives you back the right to be free and the ability to grow. Without this, you are left to work harder at co-parenting and will not be able to invest in a co-parenting system that helps all parties find a place of reconciliation.

Fathers tend to be less aware of the reasons for the relational breakdown. Hence, they are not likely to talk about the problems. Being less aware of the problems inhibits fathers from seeking post-divorce analysis, or from seeking forgiveness and remorse from their spouse.[8]

With forgiveness, you forgive your spouse and release yourself from your own cell

Women often come out of the divorce with more responsibilities and worry. Because of this, they often find it harder to let go of bad feelings. Many times, they are not free to move because of a feeling of inequality at the outcome of the divorce.

Sharing blame about the divorce is perceived differently by couples. In one study 55% of couples were found to share the blame, 31% attributed the breakup to the spouse, and men were more likely to blame the wife for the breakup. In my couple's work, fathers often did see the difficulties, but not the end coming. This would lead to a misunderstanding of who is at fault when the end comes and leaves one partner blaming the other.[8]

In addition, mothers are often expected to be the one to maintain the relationship with the extended family by networking, whereas the fathers, after the divorce, had less responsibility and had more social and recreational participation with the children. This dynamic plays an important role; mothers keep some normality in the new divorce relationship with the extended family and allow children to still belong to a piece of the old system.

After a divorce, mothers often experience greater economic hardship, which adds more pressure and anxiety. This is a time when a mother does not just get to play the role of mother but has to deal with a stressful financial situation. Not in every situation, but often the fathers enjoy an enhanced financial situation. Mothers often have had a restricted education or lack of career opportunities because of the mothering role. This changes their income perspective when a divorce happens. Mothers often will put their education on hold to start a family or for the spouse to complete theirs. In addition, a mother who has been a parent for many years and then has to enter the workforce is often not as in touch with current needs in the workforce.[8]

> *Keeping some normality in the new divorce relationship allows children to still belong to a piece of the old system.*

Regardless of gender, acknowledging and educating couples who are co-parenting about perceptual differences reinforces their differences. Rather than focusing on who is right or wrong, a victim or villain, couples can move towards a healing process and move towards a quality co-parenting relationship. We are different; no matter how hard we work to understand the other person as a parent, we will always have our differences. What we do with them is up to us. We can see our partner as a villain or our self as a victim, but divorce makes us both. Co-parenting successfully will take away the labels and allow the couple to give the love they had in the marriage to the children. In addition, it will help the parent remember the other parent was once part of the family.

We can see our partner as a villain or our self as a victim, but divorce makes us both.

CHAPTER 15

Programs for Divorcing Couples

· ·

With the onset of so many divorces there are many U.S. states that now require divorcing parents to take education classes about the impact of divorce on parents and children.[20]

For some couples, a divorce educational program is an option. Divorce is a time when a child's need for reassurance is at an all-time high.[14] A divorce education program is a way to help parents through the emotional roller coaster and help facilitate a way to improve the interaction styles of the parents. This could be a divorce workshop, an online program, a church-based divorce program or just finding educational books on the issues that are present in divorce. This intervention is aimed at a cooperative co-parenting alliance. Inter-parental problems and open conflict are two of the issue's children have to deal with when divorce is present.[14] In my divorce, I attended a divorce recovery program and, in many ways, it helped, but also showed me that my life was not so bad. Although I was going through a difficult time, there were people there that had lived with abuse and trauma in their relationship. Working on myself in this program, I was able to move faster into a better co-parenting system.

A divorce education program is a way to help parents through the emotional roller coaster.

Studies show parents that attend a divorce education program were less likely to have their children miss school and spend time in the doctor's office for divorce-related illnesses. Although an educational program helped, it did not alleviate the bad behavior of the parents, like power plays or needing too much control.

The education program discouraged negative behavior but did not increase positive experiences.[14] It is not easy to leave negative thoughts behind, but even a small shift after a recovery program is a road to starting a better family environment. Most education programs will be in groups with others that are going through many of the same issues. They often move the larger group into smaller groups for more of an intimate setting. This allows for a person to share their pain and issues without being overwhelmed by a large group.

For high conflict relationships, educational programs are one way of helping to co-parent, but another is parenting coordination. A coordinator helps implement and monitor parenting plans. With a high conflict divorce comes many levels of impasses in all areas of the relationship, not only with the care of the children. Often the courts will have lists of coordinators or appoint one.

A parenting coordinator will work with the parents in all areas of discourse, which will in turn protect the child. The coordinator helps the parents learn to communicate, resolve conflict, and keeps them focused on the children. These services are sometimes ordered by the court. However, advocating for the parents to resolve their own differences is the goal and allows both parents to feel like they are partnered with the coordinator.[5]

For high conflict relationships, educational programs are one way of helping to co-parent.

In addition, mediation can be used by the couple to engage each other. Mediators can help pull the couple together using the knowledge of family therapy. A shared parenting support program is a way to approach co-parenting skills. The early period of any divorce is filled with misunderstanding and confusion and for some the mediator helps set a goal. Laying out a road map of ideas helps couples implement them for a better outcome. Through this program, there are four immediate goals: 1. Help the parent's co-parent in a safe environment, 2. Communicate directly about the needs of the children, 3. Avoid communication through the children, and 4. Avoid placing children in the middle of the conflict. This program uses cognitive therapy and family systems theory to work towards their goals.[21]

Co-parenting questionnaires are also a way to predict and follow what is happening for children of divorce and a way to improve cooperative co-parenting. The questionnaire helps target the strengths and weaknesses as perceived by the child. With this information, the couple can see the pain and needs of their child. The outcome is the ability for the parents to view the hostility through the eyes of their children, and hopefully will motivate the parents to cooperatively co-parent.[23]

CHAPTER 16

Religion and Divorce

· ·

While religion is not always an issue during a divorce, for some families it is. Some divorced fathers are less likely to be engaged in religious socialization after the divorce.[30] Fathers might find it hard to be at a church both parents attended or might feel they would be judged by the church members. Also moving into an area unknown to the father, might be more difficult to decide what church or religious location they would want to attend. One of the reasons is that often the custody arrangement favors the mother. This is not to say the roles could not be revised. A second reason parental divorce diminishes religious involvement is feeling judged by the congregation or additionally being ostracized. In a strong, faith-based family, it is hard to reconcile with a divorce. Divorce also disrupts the relationships with the extended family who may be a facilitator of religious training and commitment.[30]

The continued religious experience is important for the children after the divorce. When a father continues a religious commitment, a stronger father-child relationship develops. For the child it shows a greater parental engagement, and an investment in their lives. Children are able to see their father invested in their social and emotional development. This study reported this involvement was critical for shaping and organizational religious activities of the child.[30]

Regular church attendance is associated with a stronger bond in the family. A lack of organized religious involvement when one has been present is a factor for children and can add to how they are affected by the divorce.[30]

When a father continues a religious commitment, a stronger father-child relationship develops.

CHAPTER 17

Reorganization
Post-Divorce

· ·

How do couples reorganize themselves after a divorce? It's said divorced families need 18 to 24 months to settle and reorganize their lives.[26] The losses must be worked through, coordinating parenting, the loss of the intimate partner, and the loss of a social network associated with the former partner. The symptoms for individuals after a divorce are anxiety, depression, psychosomatic symptoms, substance abuse, and bad habits linked to physical health.

Cooperative co-parenting is "the ability to support each other in raising children for whom you share responsibility for many years after the divorce." Although some parents are successful at co-parenting, not all parents can reach this goal.[26] These are parents that amplify individual problems and make it difficult, if not impossible, to establish a relationship. It is very sad, as the only person who suffers for the rest of their life is the child.

So, what is a "good divorce?" What does work for families? The societal norm is that couples cannot speak safely to each other after a divorce; these couples become single parents. The popular expectation is when they separate, they will not be able to work together because of the conflict in the divorce or marriage. The common belief is if the couple can get along and communicate why they would have not stayed together. This is a very good question, one that society has asked and continues to ponder. There is no such thing as a single parent. The only single parent is the one that never sees the other spouse and has no contact with the children. The co-parenting partnership is the complex interpersonal task of adults sharing parenting responsibilities.[29]

It is important to separate your parental interactions from your feelings before the divorce.

LETTING GO WHILE HOLDING ON

Positive attachment between former spouses can be misunderstood, which is a sad state of affairs. Positive attachment is only friendliness and respect, which increases the ability of both to get along well AND BECOME GREAT PARENTS. Clinicians do a disservice to clients when they advise them to cut all relational ties with their former spouse. Couples can have civil, cordial interactions without this being viewed as unrealistic, reunion fantasies.[29]

> *The co-parenting partnership is the complex interpersonal task of adults sharing parenting responsibilities.*

In a good divorce, a family with children remains a family. The parents continue to care for the children as if they were married and the couple becomes a parenting partnership in —**The New Family**.[2] This partnership permits the bonds of kinship and everyone benefits when the parents communicate regularly; rules remain the same in both homes and parents support each other.[29]

In this **New Family**, mother and father enact the parenting role capably and children grow up with close ties to both parents. These parents in this new family system do not have a romantic relationship nor do they live together, but that does not mean a post divorced family cannot function as healthy as a two-parent family. One thing that is known for sure is if the divorced parents enacted the relationship of married parents, the children thrive. The next chapter will explain how that can happen.

In this New Family, mothers and fathers enact the parenting role capably and children grow up with close ties to both parents.

CHAPTER 18

Working together as The New Family

. . . .

Many things are important for the children after the dust settles and one of these is consistency. Children need to know how and why the rules apply and the rules need to be the same in both households. If both houses have the same rules, then there is no confusion for the children. If they move from one home to the other with a lack of order, it will make it hard for them to understand why it does not work in one house but does in the other. As they grow into young teens, this balance needs to be as solid as it can be! The more order and stability in both homes, the more the ability the child has to develop a sense of self.

The rules we established IN OUR HOMES AND FAMILY were:

1. *The children were never told "no" by one parent, then asked the other for the same thing, hoping for a "Yes"*

We were able to make this work; we had the same morals, beliefs, and trust that we both would do the best for the girls. Begin together, by being clear with the children that the rules apply at both houses. If one of the parents says "no," the other parent will support the "no" and reinforce the decision that was made. However, when the child would like a different outcome, this could become a problem, putting the parents against each other, and causing friction. The parents would be the ones that would change that outcome, not the individual parent going against the other. Parents need the chance to review what the request is and make a healthy choice.

This is very important and other books on parenting will advise the same. However, it goes beyond just not saying yes or no. It is about the respect the child has for the parent. If a child believes both parents have respect for each other, then the request goes without saying. Many children who do not see parents respecting each other will play one off against the other. In addition, the child will do this even if they don't want to get their way just to get attention and to punish.

Children that think the parents are making them feel unimportant will act out to get attention, like disobeying or ignoring their parent's requests, lying and more. What are the children learning here? That rules are fluid? How can you then expect to have the child comply with other requests? How do they conform to societal norms if they don't start with the very people that are the closest to them?

The parents would be the ones that would change that outcome, not the individual parent going against the other.

2. *Taking time off school had to be agreed upon by both parents*

As with my girls who are both bright, smart, and moving on in life with a strong conviction to education, leaving and going to England during the school year did not set them back. But it made it easier for me to go when the fares were cheaper or at times that the family in England had major events. This was often where we as parents found it harder to agree, but we were able to work it out. Not all co-parenting in a divorce is easy, BUT not all two parenting is easy either!

Often parents will have times when there are activities or family requirements that interfere with the school schedule. Depending on the age of the child, attendance in school can be more or less important. It does not always work out, but if possible, parents need to make it work. It is necessary to have both parents discuss this and not decide based on hurting the other parent. This can be a very "sticky wicket" (a cricket term). However, it makes for a better relationship if one of the parents can compromise. It is not always easy to let go of what you believe. If you believe not one school day should be missed, then it is going to be a struggle when this comes up. Baring major exams and tests, children will catch up. However, all children are different and learn differently, so knowing your child and communicating with the other parent is important. It is not the end of the world to let elementary children go to a wedding in another state or country and miss a week or two of school.

> ### Not all co-parenting in a divorce is easy, BUT not all co-parenting in a marriage is easy either!

3. *Joining groups, sports, and activities were agreed upon by both parents and the organization of these activities was a family issue. What was the cost, how were they getting there, who was going to be responsible for the details?*

For our girls, there were only a few times they belonged to a sport or activity. However, when they wanted to join karate or a high school band, we worked out how we would make it work as a family. It was about working through the details, even on days that were not technically "our day," we would make sure the child got to where they needed to be.

Your children will more often go in and out of activities as they go through different stages of development. At times one parent might want the child to stay and the other want to stop the sport or event. This is where both parents need to work together, including the child, in the conversation to see what is needed for the good of the child. Many divorced parents fight over the fees. It becomes "I am going to win this one." Well, it is not a game or about winning; it is what is best for the children. It is also a time that control comes into play. It is an opportunity for one of the parents to get one-up on the other. BAD MOVE! How sad that a hobby or a joy your child has become a ploy to hurt your former partner. Co-parenting encourages a harmonious environment when these issues are addressed and worked through together. Having a parent miss an activity by not informing them to make a point only hurts the child!

It was about working through the details, even on days that were not technically "our day."

4. *Share the children's achievements with the grandparents and extended family on both sides*

For us, it was never a question. Our girls never missed a family event. It was always about building a loving relationship with the grandparents and extended family. Even when there was a conflict, the grandparents came first. Now that the children are grown, I have no regrets and feel grateful that they were able to be such a big part of both our extended families and have experienced all the memorable moments.

The grandparents did not ask for the divorce or ask to miss seeing their grandchildren in events. Moreover, they are not in the mix of co-parenting. They are and will always be their grandparents. Making room for them is important for the development of the family, even if it clashes with your custodial time. Having the children spend time with them when they have an event or important occasion should be accommodated by both parents. Allow for the grandparents' birthdays and special occasions to be about the children. Invite the grandparents to events, not just when the children are with one parent.

Putting barriers up will only create discord and build unhappiness for the children. In the big picture, making the children miss something they wanted to be at with the grandparents will only make them resent the parents. The resentment can carry over to when they get older, causing tension in the relationship!

It was always about building a loving relationship with the grandparents and extended family.

5. *Questions that were difficult to answer by one parent were asked of the other to help find the right answer.*

In my relationship, both of us took time to talk through difficulties that the children had and at times would defer to each other as the best person to deal with the situation. We would talk whenever we needed to and navigated many situations for the better. It was not a competition. Don't make it one!

You are not alone; parenting is a team. Although the team is now "The New Family" team, it is there to be used. No one must figure out all the answers alone, as you have each other to work through the different stages of the child's life and the questions that might present themselves based on the situation at the time. There are big questions and small ones, but all the questions will be for the two of you. A child might want to share with their mother or father things that just belong between that specific pair. This is part and parcel of growing up.

At different stages in a child's life, one parent over the other becomes more important. Girls will want their mother and then need their fathers. Boys would want their father then need their mothers. We move in a fluid situation in divorce, which we need to understand. They might even want to move in with the other parent at some time. This is all part of growing up and children often need a different environment to try out.

It was not a competition.

6. *Not keeping secrets from each parent unless it was a birthday present!*

Sometimes the girls would want to tell their dad something and tell him not to tell me. Dads and daughters have that bond. However, if he felt I needed to know for the good of the girls, then he would tell me with the opening "Please don't tell them I told you." Knowing something that I could change about myself, or what I was doing, was only going to help my relationship with the girls; It was more important that I knew. There were times when it was painful, as I did not want to be a bad parent or not doing my job. But the girls felt safe telling dad stuff that I might have been off course with, and by telling him it gave him a chance to help me be a better parent. It is not easy being told by your former spouse that you are messing up! But it only made for a better household for the children. I was able to do the same with him and he did not listen all the time, but that is part of relationships whether you are married or divorced.

It is not easy being told by your former spouse that you are messing up.

7. *Sharing fears about the children and at times our own fears*

I had fears, I believe we all do as parents and individuals. We have children and hope we do the best. However, we bring our own history into parenting and our own losses. When working together, there were times that fear got the better of both of us. I felt some of my questions and worry could only be understood by the other parent. We both wanted to be as healthy as we could for the best of the family and children.

When a parent has a fear and keeps it to themselves, it is hard to know what is going on and the other parent or child might just come up with their own conclusions. Often a child might feel they are at fault. Not all things need to be shared with the children, but parents can still depend on each other for support. Honesty is a very important part of co-parenting.

> ## We both wanted to be as healthy as we could for the family and children.

8. *If a new partner is now part of the family, then include all members to be together if the children want it. If not, think about whether it really matters if the new person is included. Or is this time about the children, and not your new life?*

This was the hardest time for us as a family. New partnerships can often bring their own unique difficulties. Sometimes a new partner may not have experience being a parent or sharing a family. We did not work it out as well as we could have, but in time it did become easier and as the girls got older, they became needier of their father's time, which changed the family unit.

At this junction, it must be done slowly and with the kids at the forefront. It does not matter what you want and how much you want a new relationship, or you are lonely or just want to be in a relationship. Doing this slowly is going to be best all the way around. The children need to be on board, as they must believe you care about them more than the new person. You can do this by not letting them down when they ask you for something that is important to them and also by realizing that they are not always being demanding but are often just need to feel safe in the family. For an adult or a parent, it is not easy to understand the emotions of a child. They don't operate from the same logic or understanding. They are yours, and only you can make them feel safe. You do this by being open to not having it your way in the new relationship, and putting the needs of the children first. Yes, it can be done, but you must realize that you are not as important as their security and safety. We all want to be happy, but happiness must come from being a parent first and foremost.

At this junction, it must be done slowly and with the kids at the forefront.

9. *Become friends*

This is not as hard as it seems, but I do understand how couples say, "Never going to happen." We did not have adultery, addiction, or abuse in the marriage; hence, we were able, after the court and the pain was decreasing, to become friends. I made it a point to share first and to keep the channel open. We were able to work on talking and then visiting each other in each other's homes. After about a year, we started eating together and working on even taking the girls on a vacation together. It became easier and had a positive effect on our girls.

This has to be mutual, but one person must make the move to break through the ugly and work on building reconciliation. It won't happen unless you understand it is for the good of the future family and YOU. No one needs to live with hate or anger. You can unload and make a new path for YOU, and that makes a new path for everyone in the family. How bad would it be to be friends with the one person that you are going to spend the rest of your life knowing? You will be together at every important function that your children will be at—graduations, weddings, births? Would it not be better if you were friends?

> *How bad would it be to be friends with the one person that you are going to spend the rest of your life knowing?*

CHAPTER 19

Program for a Better Co-Parenting

. . . .

First and foremost, you must love your child more than you dislike your spouse. YES, I AM A BROKEN RECORD, I keep saying this, as it is so important and the beginning of healing and change.

These children did not ask to be in this situation and as divorce becomes more common, figuring out what works in the best interest of the child is the focus.

Reconciliation

Yes, reconciliation is possible even if it seems like it can never happen, but it can. It has to be when you are ready and have gone through the steps of understanding, acceptance, and forgiveness.

You had a role in the divorce whether you filed or you did not. Adultery, as hard as it is to hear, is not a singular act. In a broken or damaged marriage, adultery happens. It is not right and is not the right course of action when a person feels alone in a relationship but is often the outcome.

I remember one evening very late, during that first year of my divorce, I could not sleep and could not stop thinking about my role in the relationship. It was not easy to own my part, but my part was there. I played out how I had helped get to the point of this breakdown and decided that to own it was a way for me to let go.

First and foremost, you must love your child more than you dislike your spouse.

I went down and woke my spouse and told him I was sorry. I was sorry for all the times I had been mean, the times I had pushed him to his limits, the times I could only see my point of view. It was a good moment and a moment in my life I will never forget. It made me a better person and allowed me to believe that I could be free of hurt and anger.

The court orders visitation and custody, but in a good relationship the kids should be able to spend time with both parents. It works when they can move around within the two households and share their time when needed and not having to keep secrets about each home as the other parent might get angry. For a child, it is a relief to just be themselves without worry. Keeping the rigidity in the court order only makes life hard for the children. A respect for each other's times and needs as two adults is what is needed.

For me, I went back to school for 11 years and had to change my times with the children every semester. Sundays I did my homework and wrote my papers. When I had time off, they would stay with me more and when I was busy they would be at their father's. At all three of my graduations, BA, MA and Doctorate, we were there as **The New Family**.

Kids should be able to spend time with both parents.

Extended Family

Extended family is often very important at the end of a marriage. Many children find this is where they feel the safest. However, there are situations when extended family can be stressful. We know that everyone is affected by divorce and the extended family relationships are not the exception. There are two sets of extended families and both sides need to remember this. Often after a divorce, there is a higher level of closeness to your own family. However, the number of years married influences the post-divorce relationship with the extended family.

Hence, they must know that the extended family is still part of their family. Working to keep all the pieces together is an important job. If the extended family is kept out of the drama of the breakup, then it is easier. However, if they were part of the coalition on one side or the other, this will have to be worked through. Most in-laws want to stay neutral and care for the children the best they can.

> *There are two sets of extended families and both sides need to remember this.*

Many divorced parents will lean on the in-laws for support not only to help with the children but also to help keep some stability in the parents' life. It is good for the children to be aware that this bridge is still intact. When the in-laws add fuel to the fire of the couple's divorce, then there needs to be a plan on both the parents' sides to help bridge this gap.

One way to help make this work is by being understanding and generous when it comes to in-law time. Many couples that have a legal court order for visitation will not budge on a grandparent's birthday or event. In addition, the parent might even make it harder for the grandparent to see the children.

It is best if you consider how much your children love their grandparents and work hard to keep that at the forefront until the kids can make their own decisions about seeing their grandparents.

Working together as <u>The New Family</u>

This part of the journey starts when all the hurt has subsided. That does not mean you are suddenly, miraculously, and spontaneously different. YOU are still the person that has gone through a major life change and has obstacles in their path, but you should want the best for the children.

Helping each other out

- Jumping in when you can if need be
- Changing plans to work for the kids or even your ex-spouse
- Keeping an open mind to what each other needs
- Don't put obstacles in the other parent's path so that they must jump through hoops

With all the data, we can see what works and what doesn't work with the divorced family. What is missing is the ingredients that make the cooperative family tick. The wrongs acted out in divorce are very clear and consistent. Children do not ask for a divorce, but according to all the studies they are paying for this breakdown in the family and the marriage. Research is still needed to find out what parts of success are in THE NEW FAMILY and a way to put these parts together to create a safe and healthy place to live.

Throughout the book, I write about being past the hurt. This takes work and is not easy, but as a parent, you can do it. YOU CAN, YOU HAVE TO WANT TO.

CHAPTER 20

Christmas, Holidays, and Events in The New Family

. . . .

Once we were past the hurt, we worked on how to do the holidays for the kids. In my case, it was different, as my family all lived in England and his family lived in the area. We decided to spend Christmas with his family. This was not hard for us, as at that time we were both single and willing to keep the same patterns for the kids. We had worked past the hurt and now wanted teamwork.

When married if a couple has two sets of in-laws staying locally, then they would have developed a pattern that worked for them. This is the pattern that you would want to try and keep intact. Some will say this would confuse the kids, but if they are aware that the relationship is over, then doing this can be part of the two of you both getting along, which invariably will help the children transition into the new norm.

Making Christmas Work

We would meet at the mall with the kids before Christmas. Each child would go off with one parent to shop. We shopped for each other, for the kids, and had fun just deciding what to buy. The kids would have ideas of what to give us and what they believed the other parent might want. There was an excitement that kept the joy in Christmas for the kids. This was not about us; it was about the children and it was a tradition we kept until they were old enough to not care about shopping for the parents! Every year each daughter went with the same parent and did a great job of having fun. We would eat together after shopping. When they were younger, they would have fun trying to drop hints as to what the gifts were or go to great lengths to hide the gift at the table!

Christmas presents for both girls were purchased by me. The amount spent was agreed on and avoided the girls getting two sets of gifts. We also wanted them to understand we were on the same page. The gifts would have meaning, as they came from both of us, and was not a competition of who could buy the most or the best.

As we both had parents, mine in England and his local, we did, on some occasions, spend Christmas apart. I would take them to England, but we would make sure Christmas morning we included their father in the festivities from afar.

The gifts would have meaning, as they came from both of us and was not a competition of who could buy the most or the best.

In addition, on Christmas in the early years and because he lived so close, their father would come over to my house in the morning before they were up, so when they came down he would be there to share the excitement.

It is understandable when a relationship is over, and a couple has started a new family to figure out how that works. Many times, it can work out the way we did. However, if that does not work at least the children could have time with both parents during the shopping phase.

Now you might ask how strange it is to be buying your ex-spouse a Christmas gift, but that is not what is happening; although you do end up with a gift, the kids are learning that it is possible to have two parents that don't have to be mean to each other and care. It demonstrates that we were working as a team and that the family unit is a priority, regardless of the divorce.

Think about it, why should you not care for a person you decided to marry, have children with and then end the relationship? You are done when you divorce with the intimacy of the relationship, but do you really have to hate the other person? Is that really the next step? Or can it become an understanding that you are joined for the rest of your life when you have children?

The obstacles to being able to work this into a successful Christmas can be new relationships. Part of understanding how to co-parent successfully is having worked with your new partner and helped them understand that you are still a parent, but also their new partner. Insecurity towards an old spouse is often through fear and misunderstanding. It is important to both understand your role as a parent and to have agreed that the children and their well-being must come first. If not, the road will be a difficult one.

I believe communicating what is expected in the beginning will help. However, this must be done honestly and with the facts and perimeters that work for the children.

It demonstrates that we were working as a team and that the family unit is a priority, regardless of the divorce.

Children's Birthdays

This is a special day for the kids and why should it not be! They are turning another year older and that means a lot to most kids. They want to spend this day with people they love and care about. It is important for this one day of the year that it is all THEIRS to not be about the parents. There is no reason why the kids cannot have both parents together. It would be because of your own difficulties that it would not work, not because of the kids. This one day is for a child you bought into this world that loves you both.

> ## It is important for this one day of the year that it is all THEIRS.

Having Meals Together

Sharing meals together is something that we did, and for sure would not be easy for everyone. However, we both stayed single for many years, which helped. It was not uncommon for the girls to say, "Shall I see if dad wants to eat?" He would come over after work and eat, or sometimes just pop in to see how their day went. In addition, there were times that he would cook and invite me to eat too. It was never anything but two parents enjoying their children. We might not have been married anymore, but we were still the parents of these two girls. I believed we made it work, as this was more important than being angry at each other. We had come through the difficult time of adjusting, the time of blaming each other, and now we had gotten to the point of enjoying being parents. It can be done; you just have to want it enough and exert the effort. Being together for a meal out is also acceptable and works. Not all time spent with the children and former spouse should include a new relationship. However, this is again where the understanding that the new relationship is safe and eating with the kids and their mother is not about going back or abandoning the new relationship but giving the kids some family time.

....

*It can be done; you just have to want
it enough and exert the effort.*

....

For many, this will seem bizarre and awkward and this situation after a divorce might seem strange. But this is something that can happen because you can work together as a team, and the fear from the new relationship has been addressed. No one leaves a relationship undamaged; working on healing is about you.

School functions

When it comes to the school system, it is so important that the children have you there together. So many children have suffered from trying to navigate parents coming at different times. Children have enough stress trying to do well at school without investing in the situation of divorce.

Teacher conferences should be with both parent's present. This is a good way to start working together in the early stages. For one, the teacher does not have to worry about trying to make it work, and second, the child can have the pride of seeing both their parents admire their work together as a team. What a sad situation it has become when a child must worry their parents might cross paths. Does a child not have the right to be just that and not the negotiator of two adults? The school system has contributed to making this situation worse by not having one meeting, as they fear the situation and have now conformed to this system.

With one meeting in mind, parents would have to stay respectful of each other in this situation and would not be able to make themselves look bad. Imagine what that would be like for a child to see you both together? Not just together, but not at odds at an important time in their school life.

Not only do teacher conferences affect the children but also any kind of performance where they want their parents to be proud of them. To look up and see both your parents together is an amazing feeling for a child.

It is not about you being back together as an intimate couple, but about the fact that they have the two of you. It is not hard to understand a child's needs. Children are simple- It is the adult that complicates the world the child lives in. Relationships do end, but not the one with the parent if it is preserved in safety, love, and nurturing.

My children's father was present when he could be. Because he was self-employed, he sometimes had to miss functions; however, this was not because he wanted to avoid me, but because work got in the way. Moreover, the kids were always aware if dad was not there it was because of work. More often than not, other parents were not aware that we were divorced and sometimes we would say his house or my house, and they would look at us and ask why we had two houses. We would then tell them we were divorced! You see, it does NOT have to be adversarial.

We were able to sit together at every performance our children were in and enjoy our children together. We were not in a competition or wanted to outdo the other at these times; it was about the child that we both respected and loved. Why does that have to be difficult? Could a parent not give up the ugly for a short period of time to be in JOY and PRIDE? YOU GET ONE SHOT AT PARENTING AND GIVE UP SO MUCH BY MAKING THE SITUATION ABOUT YOU!

We were not in a competition or wanted to outdo the other at these times.

In later years when the children's dad added a relationship, things did change. However, we had a foundation for working together. In all honesty, this was a tough time, and we had a difficult time getting back on track. It took time for me to be more understanding and for him to stop worrying so much about what the new partner thought. It is harder if the new partner does not have children, as they have no idea what it is like to have that relationship and expectation as a parent.

For many couples, this is a transition, and how you navigate this transition is important. This is where the transitioning parent entering a new relationship must be honest, strong, and believe in what is in the best interest of the children.

At this time in your life, it is not about you, it is about the children. They did not choose to be born and as parents, we are so lucky to have them. It is our responsibility to see what they need, through their eyes. If the job is done well, there will be a safe and happy transition. However, if the incoming new person does not have a good understanding of what the children need, then it will be a competition and both sides lose out.

The children will lose the most, as they have the most invested. How hard would it be to slow down and think about what you are doing before you jump into a new relationship? You have not left the old one behind as now you have children.

> **At this time in your life, it is not about you, it is about the children.**

For many couples entering a new relationship, this is the hardest juggling act. Unless both partners are healthy and adjusted, it can be messy. For this reason, dating should be done with a criterion that works for the family. In life, there are healthy future partners that can understand this role and will work with you to be a good parent first. You must ALWAYS realize the children did not choose this path and need both parents.

Wanting a new partner is wonderful, but not at the expense of the children. This is a time when so many couples wear blinders!

It is the most difficult of transitions and the most important. What you do at this stage can alter the life of your child for good and they will live with an insecure attachment. They may be angry and disruptive; the transition will not go smoothly. Many couples I have spoken to have said their child is just acting out but have no plan on how to integrate a new partner and not alienate the child. I cannot overemphasize the importance and time frame of this transiting conversation. More damage is done at this time than at any other.

Some couples have done a good job. I talk to children that have grown up with a stepparent they love and also love their own parents. It is possible but work must be done!

Moving on to a new relationship with no pre-planning makes for a bad relationship with your child.

In my relationship, it was not navigated as smoothly as it could have been. Primarily because the work of understanding how our lives were going to change was not discussed and worked through. Questions were not addressed and answered. Children are not considered and included. It is not enough to tell a child that someone is going to be coming into their lives, as for many children this means they will have to move over or not be important anymore. Life is going to change AGAIN and maybe they have not healed from the first change yet!

The child would have already felt the pain and loss from the divorce and to add fuel to this emotion will only end in hardship FOR EVERYONE.

Working together is the recipe for a good divorce. There are so many changes and difficult times, I understand that having been there, but working towards a better life as parents is a great choice. Twenty years later, I realize that the work we did, which was not always easy, has worked. We are proud parents of two great young women. They love both of us and think nothing of sharing with us both the joys and difficult times. Dad or Mom stories don't have to be guarded; they can be shared with us. We share our lives still today and live a full life as **The New Family**.

CHAPTER 21

Divorce Diaries

· ·

The Joy and Painful Stories from the Children of Divorce

The narratives of divorce often come from the parents, leaving their children's voices unheard. These stories document the children's narratives, how they saw their role and the role of their parents. By looking at divorce from the viewpoint of these children, my hope is that you see how your own child might feel in a similar situation. These stories are true and have the emotions and behaviors of the kids in the middle of a breakup. It is not all bad as they have stated. The resolute and understanding children can bring to a breakup is also rewarding. Children have very strong feelings and often keep them to themselves. These stories are stories of children willing to share their journey in their own words. Their names have been changed, but their emotions are present.

Amanda

Although I don't remember too much about the earlier years of the divorce, my parents have told me a little bit about it. I was told that they divorced when I was about three and my older brother (from my mom's previous marriage), Tom, was about nine.

After the divorce, they shared custody and I would go back and forth between the two of them. It was tough for the first few years, but it eventually became the norm. Communication between my parents was still very good, and although they would bicker about small things, I don't remember any big fights.

When I was in first grade, my dad introduced me to his new girlfriend. Her name was Maria. She was also divorced and had two kids. I liked Maria and her children, and it was fun hanging out with all of them, but they broke up after a while. My dad never spoke to me about the breakup, nor did it really affect me in any way.

A couple of years later, at my ninth birthday party, my dad introduced me to my now stepmom, Sarah. She has always been very kind and nice to me. We all lived together under one big roof and when I was 11, my dad told me that Sarah was pregnant with my little brother Robbie. At first, I didn't like the idea, as I liked being a single child, but I got used to it and have been very happy hanging out with him. When Robbie turned two and I was 13, they got married.

I would share a room with the eldest sibling, which was our stepsister Emily, and my brother would share a room with our stepbrother. I didn't mind the change that much because I had so much fun having other siblings and a cool garage.

My mom married John and not long into the relationship she sent me to live with my grandma. I liked John and felt we were a family. She told me that John (my stepdad) was an alcoholic and she didn't want me to be around him.

After a few years, they got a divorce. For me it was sad, as I was getting attached to this man and now I had to un-attach again! I was lost to what my role was. How was I to have any stability? All that I had adjusted to was gone again. I now feared attaching to anyone else. That's when I met my current stepdad, Steve. My mom introduced me to him as a friend originally and it eventually developed into a romantic relationship.

This helped create the bond between Steve and me. However, once we moved in with him, I started to get feelings of jealousy towards Steve. Soon they announced that they were going to get married. I was very upset as I found out about the wedding through a family friend that I went to school with. I never really showed it to my mom because she was happy, and everyone was happy, but I do remember the anger I felt. As always, I had guilt for feeling that I should have more! Mom was making sure she had what she wanted, and I had to adjust again. I just wanted her to focus on me, and not on every man that she could find. How could I attach again when this one would leave?

After they got married, I warmed up to Steve again and accepted him as my stepdad. I worked on not allowing my feelings to be important. Mom was going to do what she wanted and that was find another replacement. I felt like I could not warm up until I felt safe that he was not going to leave too. I also had to put my feelings of wanting my mom to want me more to one side and go with her plan again.

Throughout all the moving and relationships, my parents have kept in close contact so that they can help manage me and my life. They are both very loving and caring and have always kept me in mind no matter their differences. I now see myself in three different kinds of families: one between my dad, Sarah, and Robbie; one between my mom, Steve, and Tom; and one between my mom and dad.

Although it can confuse me at times and make me question my place, they all make me feel at home somehow.

Ivy

My parents divorced when I was six or seven years old. At the time I didn't know what it meant but the first thing I could remember about it was from the first day of second grade. My mom was moving out and she was putting all her stuff in a U-Haul truck. I was wearing my school uniform waiting to go to school in the front yard just watching my mom move out.

After that, I remember my mom and me living together in a single-bed apartment and not seeing my dad as often as I saw my mom. When I did go to my dad's house, my grandma would come over to help cook dinner and take care of me.

I don't know the exact time length but soon after the divorce while my mom and I were still living in the apartment, she said that she wanted me to meet someone and that was her friend. That was the first time I met her new boyfriend and ever since that moment he's been in my life. At first, I didn't know what it meant that he was with my mom; I probably just thought they were friends. A few weeks after the first meeting, he brought over his two daughters (ages seven and 12) to the apartment.

I don't remember a lot from the first time we met but I know I didn't dislike them. During this time, I remember every interaction my parents had in person was always bad; they would always argue about something and yell at each other and fight.

The fights would usually happen when my mom would pick me up from my dad's place. Over time, me and my dad would go on trips and bond more than my mom and me. I think the reason why I felt this way was because I had my dad's full attention, while with my mom she seemed fixated on her new boyfriend and his kids.

Over the years, my mom and I moved a lot and her boyfriend didn't move in for a while, but we still saw him a lot. Finally, my mom moved into an apartment and he moved in with us and I don't remember how I felt about it. But as I spent more time with the boyfriend and his daughters, one daughter (the same age as me) and I got into a lot of fights and didn't like each other. Over the years as we both got older, we had our moments where we hated each other or were best friends.

My dad soon started dating a woman when I was around 12 years old. I do remember that I was not happy about it and I hated it. Even still today I have my uncertainties about her, but I'm working to be mature with her. My dad's new girlfriend had a daughter a year younger than me and I've always liked her.

My parents dating those people has been hard for me; my mom's relationship was not a healthy one and it was hard watching constant fighting and abuse for more than 10 years.

My dad's relationship wasn't unhealthy, but I didn't like the fact I no longer could bond with him like we did before.

Christmas was hard; every year I'd switch which parent I'd spend Christmas Eve and Christmas Day with. It was always a challenge because for Christmas Eve I would be with one parent and celebrate with that side of the family and then hurry and rush on Christmas Day to see the other parent and their family. Birthdays usually depended on if I wanted to spend it with my mom or dad and every year it was different. I would always talk to both and if I didn't see one parent for my birthday, we would just celebrate another day.

Holidays for a while depended on who I was with that year and that changed every year. As I got older, I didn't want to be on a schedule anymore. The schedule determined who I was with for the weekend, so I started to go with the parent that I wanted to go with instead of the schedule.

I believe because of what I've seen and gone through, it makes me a stronger woman. I felt the need to go into therapy to express my feelings about the people my parents dated and the weak relationship I had with my parents because I believed I was blocked by the new spouses. I felt this way for a long time. I am now 17 and working on building a strong relationship with both my parents, but I won't forget how hard it was and want to put it behind me.

Jack

My parents divorced when I was three years old, and it has not been easy. I went to my dad's house and to my mom's on the schedule that was set by the court. During my time at each house, I know they did not like each other, and it was hard as they talked about each other. I wanted to block my ears and shout, "STOP." Both of my parents got remarried and had kids. It was not the same after Mom had a baby. The baby came home, and everything was different. I was now too loud; I was in the way at times. I was happy to have a baby brother, but I wanted my mom to want me as much as she did before. My stepdad changed too. I feel he loved the baby more now and I was just in the way. At dad's house, it was not as bad, as his new wife had children and they did not have a new baby. I don't think either one of my parents realized how sad I was at times and how lost I felt. I was in the middle of their lives now and at times I felt invisible. The worst time was the fights my parents still had. Dad was worse. He would threaten my mom with stopping the child support and constantly said he was taking Mom back to court. This only made my stepfather angry, and they fought over what to do. My mom was anxious and at times got angry with me, as she wanted me to stop my dad threatening her. I loved my dad but feared him. I spent a lot of time in my room and waited to grow up so I could make my own decisions and not feel like I had to please them both or hide.

Claire

My parents would argue every so often before the divorce. As a child, I'd brush it off as something that all couples did and didn't think much of it. But when I was around 13, it became clear that there were some serious issues in their marriage. The arguing had started to become more prevalent. I always tried to stay out of it and do my own thing, but after a while it became hard. It soon felt like I had to pick a side. They were both making such bold accusations towards each other and it felt like I was a judge in a case I knew nothing about. I really didn't know who was in the right, but with the serious accusations towards one another; it felt like there had to be one person in the right. During this period, I started to become colder as a person. Logically, it felt like a good way to cope with their fighting. If their fighting made me feel emotionally unstable, I would just numb my feelings towards that instability.

Throughout the year the arguments continued building up, on and off. Until one night it finally seemed to hit a climax. My mom was in tears and she finally mentioned that she wanted a divorce. This scared me to my core.

As I listened to them discuss the possibility of divorce, I had a panic attack at the thought of them leaving me. I was breathing very quickly, and I started to think much more irrationally. At that time, I saw their divorce as a life-changing experience. I felt like everything I've known and experienced from our family dynamic was in jeopardy. I was panic-stricken at the thought of that. In hindsight, it wasn't that dramatic, but it still posed a challenge that had to be dealt with. Soon after that argument, my mom moved out and took me with her and the unofficial divorce had begun.

The first year of my parents adjusting to co-parenting felt mixed. The good thing I can greatly respect my parents for in their co-parenting was their value on my stability. When my mom moved houses, she made sure not to move too far away from my school. So, despite the sudden change in my life, it didn't have that big an impact on me as a person. I still had my friends and my school in my life, and that really helped me anchor myself as a person. I finally started opening up to my parents about the divorce and I think that helped me overcome my problems with their divorce. My parents also really prioritized my well-being throughout the process; they always made sure to put me first when discussing their issues, and I knew they loved me. I'm still thankful that my parents kept that stability in my life. If things would've changed more, I'm sure the divorce would've had a greater impact on my mental well-being.

However, a criticism I have of their co-parenting would be their tendency to use me as a diplomat to communicate. Immediately after the divorce, my dad took it a lot harder than my mom.

Around the time they got divorced, he was having financial troubles with his business, so this led to a more strained relationship with him. Whenever I would spend time with him, he'd only bring up the divorce and it felt really soul sucking. He and my mom stopped communicating over the phone and it suddenly became my duty to relay information between the two.

It felt like nothing had changed from before the divorce; my parents were fighting a proxy war and the winner was the one who had my sympathy. Both my parents still would make accusations towards each other, and I was put in a spot where I had to argue for the other one's actions.

It was very frustrating for me because I loved both and it was very hard for me to hear them talk badly about each other constantly. There was a time when I didn't want to go out with my dad anymore because of how often he brought up the divorce, and how he continued to demonize my mom. He told me that my mom was "brainwashing" me and I couldn't trust her anymore, and what really made me angry about it was him insisting I would understand when I was older, implying that I couldn't grasp what he was telling me at that moment.

Ironically, my mom said the same thing about my dad, calling him a manipulative liar who wanted me to see his view instead of hers. My mom wasn't as bad in this sense, but it still felt very frustrating. I had a firm understanding that I wasn't the cause behind their divorce, but their insistence on bringing it up really made me fed up with the entire thing. After a while of dealing with it, I decided that I've had enough.

While it still irks me that I don't know who is right or wrong, I finally realized that it wasn't my place to decide that. As a judge in their case, I decided to leave the courthouse and let them figure it out on their own. I made them communicate more and leave me out of it for my own sake. And it ended up working for the most part.

Soon after my dad started seeing another woman. While they were dating, I really didn't want to meet her face to face. It felt like I didn't want to interfere in their relationship early on and I was uncomfortable with that. However, after my dad finally got married, he gradually introduced me to his wife.

At first, I was very opposed to being in my dad's new family, but he took it slow, and eventually, I started to somewhat fit in. He and his new wife seem to have a much more open relationship, which looks to last. This has probably been the easiest transition for me, as he was no longer alone and desperate for my emotional support because he had someone else to talk to.

Whenever we're together, he seems more emotionally stable than before and I think that it greatly helped our relationship. I used to feel that I never had a relationship with my dad before the divorce; he often saw me as a child, and from that point of view it felt like I could never express myself as a teenager whenever I was with him.

This really frustrated me because I value honesty in people, and it felt like he was putting up some persona whenever he was talking with me. However, in the past couple of years, I've noticed him starting to open up to me more, which I really appreciate.

I really respect my dad a lot more for taking the time to learn more about me and changing for the better. With college around the corner, it feels like my family is finally starting to smoothen out emotionally. I think that divorce is a very crucial cornerstone of a child's life. If parents are willing to work together and put their children first, I think that effort will be worth it in the end for their child's well-being.

Jessica

I have had the fortune of experiencing both the good and the bad. My parents got divorced when I was about five years old. My mum was the one who told us; she sat me and my siblings down on the floor of the living room and explained that "mummy and daddy were getting a divorce but that doesn't change their love for each other or their love for us." It was after this that my story splits into one good experience and one bad. I'll start with the good.

As we understand it now, my mum had been having an affair towards the end of her marriage, which meant she was straight into another relationship after the divorce (obviously this was not explained to us until we were older). You might expect this to create a quick turnaround and to be jarring for us children, but it was handled in such a way that negated the speed and formed a smooth and slow progression.

We were first introduced to Charles (her then-boyfriend) in very small doses—a coffee here, a lunch there—and these introductions had a heavy focus on building a friendship between us and him. My mum and Charles would give us their full attention during these introductions (playing games, doing coloring with us, asking us lots of questions, etc.) and they were never physically intimate with each other in front of us.

We were never left alone with Charles and he was not treated as an additional parent; it felt more like the relationship you have with close family friends or aunts/uncles. There was minimal pressure on us to "like him," but we inevitably did because he was so nice to us! He and my mum gave us a lot of attention when he was around, and it was always a fun experience. Slowly, our exposure to him grew, and once we felt very comfortable with him, he took on more independent parental tasks like picking us up from school, etc.

About six months after this, my mum told us that we were going to move in with Charles and both my siblings and I were very excited (I believe I was around seven at this point). From this point forward, Charles became a second dad to us; he and my mum got married and have now been together for over 20 years. He has been a huge rock in my life and can't help but well up while writing this out of pure love and gratitude for him.

I tell this story because I believe the fact that my mum and stepdad allowed us to take things slowly with Charles had a huge impact on our long-term relationship with him. I'm sure they wanted to move quickly and push us into having a relationship ASAP so they could move their relationship along, but they didn't. They put our needs first. We (the children) were always considered, we were never pushed out of our comfort zone or pressured to feel something that wasn't there. We were respected and considered key parts of the family, and for this I am so grateful.

Now for the bad, and in many ways the mirrored opposite. My dad also had an affair at the end of his marriage to my mum (as you can see, an overall unhealthy situation). However, he and his new girlfriend (Valarie) did not take things slowly or give us any time to adapt.

My dad introduced us to Valarie very quickly and there was a lot of pressure on us to form an immediate love for her, which, to be fair, we did. I adored Valarie when I first met her because there was so much hype around us getting on well and how amazing it will be to have her in our family etc., but these feelings were very shallow. I call them mushroom feelings—they grow very quickly and die just as fast.

Once we had accepted Valarie into the family, there was a dramatic shift in her persona. I believe she needed us to give her the tick of approval for my dad to move forward, but once she had the initial tick, he was no longer paying attention to how we felt about her.

My dad traveled a lot for work so when we spent the summers with him, he would leave us alone with Valarie for a week at a time and this did not bode well for either us or her. When my dad was at home, she would fight for his attention and throw tantrums if he spoke to us at dinner instead of her. So over time, he gradually started talking to us less and less, just to keep the peace. She would reference things that my dad did while he was cheating on my mum (I presume so we'd find out he was having an affair), for example, a song would come on while we were in the car and she would say, "Oh, do you remember when you would call me when your ex-wife and kids were asleep and sing this to me" loud enough for all of us (the children) to hear.

Once they had their own kid, Neville, Valarie would use him as a pawn. She would tell my dad that he didn't love Neville as much as he loved us (the children from his marriage to my mum) because he spent more money on our education (as we were between eight and 12 years older than Neville, so had already been in education for a lot longer), so she would demand my dad take her and Neville on holidays without us to make up for it.

They would return from these trips and she would get the pictures from the holidays and put them all around the family home. There are no photos of me and my full siblings in the house.

There are so many more stories I could tell you about this woman that would have your blood-curdling. I ended up in therapy by the age of 14 because of the impact she had on me, but, in truth, the bigger impact came from my dad's neglect to take my feelings on board.

I would cry to him, tell him what she had done while he was away, talk about the impact she was having on me, and he would just brush it off. He has always struggled with conflict and he handled this crack in our family through avoidance.

I stopped seeing my dad for a while, I felt so abandoned and worthless to him. It felt like he had chosen this woman over me. They stayed together for about 15 years, but unsurprisingly ended up divorced due to the traits associated with the warning signs flagging to him over a decade ago. Since their breakup, my relationship is on the mend with my dad. We have worked hard to close some of the hurt, but he still struggles to talk openly about anything that happened and I'm not sure we'll ever be quite the same as we could have been.

The reason I tell this part of the story is to urge people to listen to your children. If they are telling you they don't feel comfortable with your partner, please don't leave them with that partner alone. Don't brush things under the carpet as if it's because they're young or they're just upset because of the split. Children are resilient. I truly believe divorce does not have to be traumatizing so if your kids are having extreme reactions, it might not be the divorce that is causing that but more likely the knock-on impacts from that divorce. These are situations you have control over.

The final part of my story is my mum and dad's relationship. This to me is the reason I am a huge believer that divorce does not have to hurt your children.

As is clear from my earlier stories, my parents did not have a very healthy marriage. Affairs on both sides will often end in tears, tantrums, and wardrobes being thrown out the window. However, throughout our lives my parents have always put their personal feelings and relationships aside for us.

To this day I've got no idea how they feel about their divorce because they never told us. I don't know if there was a lot of hurt, as they never showed us a negative side to their relationships. They only told us that they will always love each other and always love us. No matter what the situation, they worked together. They never played off one other, never spoke ill of each other, never shot snide remarks at each other. They made a big effort to always be civil and considerate and I really can't stress this enough. *They put us first.*

I have never been concerned about inviting both sets of my parents to an event. Even when I was having issues with Valarie and my relationship with my dad was rocky, my mum would under no circumstances accept me cutting my dad out of anything important (graduations, exams, etc.). She would sit down and reason with me, helping me understand my dad a bit better, and urging me to maintain a relationship with him. This kindness extended to my parents' partners. My dad would only ever say positive things about Charles and my mum would try and help me develop a relationship with Valarie.

I knew my mum and dad were on the same page, even if they didn't always agree. They would check in with each other and I would certainly never get away with a no from one and a yes from the other.

My dad and Valarie currently live in America and my Mum and Charles in England. My half-brother Neville is now at a boarding school in England and when he was seven, my dad and Valarie asked my mum to become an additional legal guardian for Neville, to help support him while he was going through school. This was next level, even for our family, so I asked my parents about it. My dad's justification is that he's seen my mum raise me and my full siblings and how amazing she is as a parental figure so there is no one he would rather trust his child with than her. My mum's justification for saying yes is that Neville is our brother, which makes him family so, of course, she would do anything she could to help.

I want to highlight this because this is the level of love that is still possible in divorced homes. I can imagine my parents have experienced bumps along the road and it isn't all sunshine and daisies. But it is still possible to have a healthy and loving home for your children after a split.

I believe having a stable relationship in my life (my mum and step-dad) and a stable partnership from my parents completely over shone the negative impacts from my dad and stepmom's relationship and the typical negative consequences of divorce. I do not wear my 'child of divorce' badge with shame. I'm proud of where I come from, the lessons my parents have taught me, both together and apart, and I truly believe divorce doesn't have to destroy a family; it merely evolves it.

Katie

I am currently experiencing the repercussions of a divorce. I switch houses weekly with both of my parents. You would think the process of divorce is over once you settle the terms of money, custody, etc., but it's the exact opposite. A divorce begins after it's over. Loss. Abandonment. Heartbreak. Words cannot describe the feeling and experience as a child when your parents get divorced. Divorce is something you think you know, but you never do until you experience it. So, here is my story. My parents decided to get divorced two years ago.

I was a sophomore in high school and my world was flipped upside down. I was born into a blended family, where I was the youngest of five kids. I grew up watching them navigate high school and relationships and experiencing what it was like to have divorced parents. Soon, they all moved out and it was my turn to take the reins. I was fortunate enough to start high school with my parents still married and all my siblings living in California. Freshman year passed, and everything went downhill. Soon by next March, my brother was moving to Texas and my parents separated. Loss. I had my life flash before my eyes and in just a month, my mom and I moved into our first apartment. I had to be the rock for our family being the youngest child. Put on a smile no matter what I was feeling. Sweep it all under the rug. No one asked if I was okay. You learn to deal with conflict internally and never to bother others with your feelings. I still live by this today. Fast forward two more years it hasn't gotten any easier.

You must worry about keeping each parent satisfied, watching them date other people, spend nights alone at home, and even worse, get engaged. As of now, my mom and I moved in with her fiancé of four months. This is where the feeling of abandonment and heartbreak comes in. It hurts to know that you are not the center of your parents' lives anymore. I must juggle everything: school, college applications, fake and healthy friendships, anxiety, and never disappointing my parents. I feel like a pawn on a chessboard. I get moved around and try not to pull baggage with me. Over the past two years, I've developed trust and abandonment issues, and never been able to fully open up to others. During it all, I've known independence, self-worth, and understand the true meaning of family. I never wish divorce for any family, since it is by far the hardest thing I've ever been through. I hope one day I experience true love and finding the person I can fully open up to. I wouldn't trade my story for anything, it has taught me to never take family for granted. My saga will continue until I leave home.

As you can read in these stories there is a common theme of abandonment and a loss of belonging. During the process of divorce, with all that must be done emotionally and physically, children often fall through the gap. A parent does not want this for their child, but without good planning and reflection it happens. I hope this book and the insights that I have covered help you see the situations, difficulties and planning that must take place for a good relationship after divorce.

RESOURCES

Reconcilable Differences: Rebuild Your Relationship by Rediscovering the Partner You Love—Without Losing You by Andrew Christensen and Brian D Doss and Neil S Jacobson

The Rules of Engagement: Rules of Engagement: Learning from Nine Couples Who Made Marriage Work by Dorothy O'Neill

Mindfulness for Chocolate Lovers by Diane R Gehart

REFERENCES

1. Ahrons, C. (1994). The Good Divorce. New York: HarperCollins.

2. Amato, P.R., Kane, J.B., & James, S. (2011). Reconsidering the 'Good Divorce'. Family Relations, 60(5), 511-524. https://doi.org/10.1111/j.1741-3729.2011.00666.x

3. Andreasson, J. & Johansson, T. (2019) Becoming a half-time parent: Fatherhood after divorce, Journal of Family Studies, 25(1), 2-17. https://doi.org/10.1080/13229400.2016.1195277

4. Arditti, J.A., & Kelly, M. (1994). Father's perspectives of their co-parental relationships post-divorce: Implications for family practice and legal reform. Family Relations: An Interdisciplinary Journal of Applied Family Studies, 43(1), 61—67. https://doi.org/10.2307/585143

5. Bacher, N., Fieldstone, L., & Jonasz, J. (2005). The role of parenting coordination in the family law arena. American Journal of Family Law, 19(2), 84.

6. Baum, N. (2003). Divorce Process Variables and the Co-Parental Relationship and Parental role Fulfillment of Divorced Parents. Family Process, 42(1), 117.

7. Bertelsen, B. (2021). Staying with the conflict – parenting work and the social organization of post-divorce conflict, Journal of Family Studies, https://doi.org/10.1080/13229400.2020.1869578

8. Bonach, K., Sales, E., & Koeske, G. (2005). Gender Differences in Perceptions of Coparenting Quality Among Ex-partners. Journal Of

Divorce Remarriage, 43(1-2), 1-28. https://doi.org/10.1300/J087v43n01_01

9. Ernst, T., & Altis, R. (1981). Joint Custody and Co-Parenting: Not By Law But By Love. Child Welfare, 60(9), 669-677.

10. Ferraro, A. J., Oehme, K., Bruker, M., Arpan, L., & Opel, A. (2018) The Impact of Training Videos on Attitudes About Parenting After Divorce, Journal of Divorce & Remarriage, 59(7), 590-600. https://doi.org/10.1080/10502556.2018.1466253

11. Gehart, D (2019). Mindfulness for Chocolate Lovers: A Lighthearted Way to Stress Less and Savor More Each Day

12. Godbout, É., & Parent, C. (2012). The Life Paths and Lived Experiences of Adults Who Have Experienced Parental Alienation: A Retrospective Study. Journal of Divorce & Remarriage, 53, 34-54.

13. Guidelines for the practice of parenting coordination. (2021). American Psychologist, 67(1), 63-71. https://doi.org/10.1037/a0024646

14. Hans, J. D., & Fine, M.A. (2001). Children of Divorce: Experiences of Children Whose Parents Attended a Divorce Education Program. Journal of Divorce & Remarriage, 36(1/2), 1.

15. Hazan, C., & Shaver, P. (1987). Romantic love conceptualized as an attachment process. Journal of Personality and Social Psychology, 52(3), 511-524. https://doi.org/10.1037/0022-3514.52.3.511

16. https://theawarenesscentre.com/parentification

17. https://www.cdc.gov/nchs/fastats/marriage-divorce.htm

18. https://www.verywellmind.com/erik-eriksons-stages-of-psychosocial-development-2795740

19. https://www.verywellmind.com/john-bowlby-biography-1907-1990-2795514

20. Kennedy, J. H., & Kennedy, C. E. (2004). Attachment theory: Implications for school psychology. Psychology in the Schools, 41(2), 247-259. https://doi.org/10-1002/pits.10153

21. Leek, D.F. (1992) Shared Parenting support program. American Journal of Forensic Psychology, 10(2)

22. Madden-Derdich, D. A., & Leonard, S. A. (2002). Shared experiences, unique realities: Formerly married mothers' and fathers' perceptions of parenting and custody after divorce. Family Relations, 51(1), 37-45.

23. Mullett, E. K., & Stolberg, A. (1999). The development of the Co-parenting Behaviors Questionnaire: An instrument for children of divorce. Journal of Divorce & Remarriage, 31(3-4), 115-137.

24. Nielsen, L. (2013). Shared Residential Custody: Review of the Research (Part II of II)

25. Sandler, I., Gunn, H., Mazza, G. et al. Effects of a Program to Promote High Quality Parenting by Divorced and Separated Fathers. Prev Sci 19, 538-548 (2018). https//doi.org/10.1007/s11121-017-0841-x

26. Togliatti, M. M., Lavadera, A. L., & Benedetto, R. D. (2011). How couples re-organized themselves following divorce: Adjustment, co-parenting and family alliance. Life Span and Disability, 14(1), 55-74.

27. Walker, J. (1993). Co-operative parenting post-divorce: Possibility or pipedream?. Journal Of Family Therapy, 15(3), 273-292. doi:10.1111/j.1467-6427.1993.00759.x

28. West, C., Hart, M. (1998). Parenting: Examining the Father. International Journal Of Childbirth Education, 13(4), 18.

29. Whiteside, M. F. (1998). The Parental Alliance Following Divorce: An Overview. Journal Of Marital & Family Therapy, 24(1), 3-24.

30. Zhai, J.E., Ellison, C. G., Glenn, N. D., & Marquardt, E. (2007). Parental divorce and religious involvement among young adults. Sociology of Religion, 68(2), 125-144. https://doi.org/10.1093/socrel/68.2.125

INDEX

ABOUT THE AUTHOR

Dorothy O'Neill is a Marriage and Family Therapist who has also worked as an adjunct professor at California State University, Northridge, Alliant International University, Irvine, and Alliant International University, Los Angeles. She has authored a book on relationships, *The Rules of Engagement: Learning from Nine Couples who make Marriage Work*. In addition, she has been published in several publications and presents on relationships and Post Trauma Stress Disorder (PTSD). Her area of specialty is in Integrated Behavioral Couples Therapy (IBCT).

She is a certified IBCT therapist and presents around the country on this topic. She has been featured on the radio and has worked to change the care for the veterans in mental health

She has a private practice in Anaheim Hills, California, specializing in couples, adolescents, trauma and military families. Her website is:

www.oneill-psychology.com